INSPIRE THE FIRE

GIVING TODAY'S YOUTH SOMETHING
Real to Believe In

RON LUCE

FOUNDER AND PRESIDENT OF TEEN MANIA MINISTRIES

CREATION HOUSE

BOOKS ABOUT SPIRIT-LED LIVING
ORLANDO, FLORIDA

Creation House
Strang Communications Company
600 Rinehart Road
Lake Mary, FL 32746
(407) 333-3132
(1-800) 283-8494
Fax (407) 333-7100

First printing, June 1994
Second printing, December 1994
Third printing, March 1995

To my daughters, Hannah and Charity.
May God give me the grace to pass on
to you the fire of His presence
that burns in my heart.

ACKNOWLEDGMENTS

So MANY PEOPLE have either directly or indirectly influenced the writing of this book.

First, I want to recognize the selfless devotion of my wife, Katie. She has not only influenced me in making me the man of God that He wants me to be, but she has allowed me to travel constantly to reach out to this broken generation. She has also been continually involved in the ministry in a number of different facets. You, truly, are the dream wife.

Joni Jones came along at just the right time to turn my writing into understandable English with correct grammar. Thank you for your commitment to excellence.

I want to thank Jim Jones and Scott Boss for sticking with me for the long haul and for picking up the slack in a big way while I was writing.

I also owe a great debt to all the staff at Teen Mania Ministries. Thank you for pouring your all out for the young generation discussed in this manuscript.

I must also express my appreciation to the Teen Mania interns of the 1993-94 season. Thank you for being the most radical examples of wild, passionate Christians I have ever seen in my life. You are truly an example of what God is raising up to take over the world!

Many people have also given favor toward the ministry over the years and have helped to make it possible to reach out to today's teens. I want to thank Willie George, Myles Munroe, Daniel Williams, David Shibley, George Babbes, Norm Mintle, Jackie Yockey, Steve Yake, Tom Newman, Billy Joe Daugherty and others who have extended their time and ministries to help us reach out to teens.

I also want to thank my colleagues in ministry — Blaine Bartel, John George, Tommy Birchfield, Lee Wilson, Eastman Curtis, Rob Koke, Gregg Johnson and many others who have shaped me as a minister of the gospel.

I would like to thank a number of Christian musicians who are attempting to reach today's teens with their music ministry and are standing with us. These include Ray Boltz, ETW, Kenny Marks, Carman, Whitecross, Kellye Huff, Petra, Eric Champion, White Heart and others who have worked with us over the years.

My earnest thanks go to all the many supporters of Teen Mania throughout the years and to all the Members of the Mandate. Thank you for putting your money where your heart is — into the generation I have described in this book. Your investment will outlive you.

To the many thousands of teens who have come on Teen Mania mission trips, thank you for being the firstfruits of a new kind of teenager in this world — willing to give up their all for the call. And to their parents, thank you all for believing in your kids and trusting us with them in the summer. Together we will make history.

Of course, most of all I want to thank my Lord Jesus Christ. Thank You for giving me a small part in the most incredible movement of the ages: Bringing mankind back to Yourself. You are my life.

TABLE OF CONTENTS

Introduction...9

Part One: Describing the Current Dilemma

1 Through the Eyes of a Teen 13

2 The Parent's Perspective 20

3 Youth Pastor's Peril..25

Part Two: How We Got Here

4 Post-Revival Parents..31

5 The Breakdown of Relationships 39

6 Nothing to Die For...51

7 Competing With the
   Razzle-Dazzle of the World..................................61

Part Three: Changing Our Perspective

8 How Does God See This Generation? 69

9 Giving Them the Vision 77

10 Believing in Their Potential 88

11 Finding Identity and Belonging in the Call.........98

Part Four: What God Is Doing With Teenagers Today

12 The Spiritual Awakening of
Teens in the Nineties.................................109

13 Real-Life World-Changers.........................122

Part Five: Where Do We Go From Here?

14 Preventive Medicine 131

15 Setting Up an Encounter With God 144

16 Providing the Opportunity.........................157

17 Living a Radical Example 165

Notes 173

Appendix 177

Y OUNG PEOPLE ACROSS America, as well as their parents and youth pastors, are caught in spiritual gridlock.

Countless churches are frequented by teens whose parents force them to go. Back pews across America are filled with teens who claim they have heard it all and so fight the boredom of weekly churchgoing with note writing, crossed arms, preacher jokes and spit-balls. They insist the hypocrisy at home is the reason for their mediocrity, but they make no effort to be an example of an on-fire Christian.

Frustrated parents keep prodding their kids to church, camps and conferences, hoping that these activities will somehow make a difference. Unaware that this creates comrades among the rebels, they add problems for the youth leaders, who cry, "We have tried everything we know to cultivate a genuine fire for God in their teens!"

Youth pastors and leaders caught in this groove of mediocrity and frustration have their own perspective. They have tried repeatedly, but it seems they just can't break through the grip the world has on some of their youth.

Even frequent "parents' meetings" bring only the parents whose kids are on fire. In one-on-one en-counters with other parents, youth leaders are unable to convince parents of the importance of bringing their teenagers to all the activities and events which have been designed to awaken the spiritual fervor of the kids. The ultimate bomb occurs when real revival breaks loose at a youth event, but the kids for whom it was planned were busy doing something else that weekend.

We must find a way out of this gridlock. Everyone would agree it's not working the way it should. How can we expect a generation of unfocused prodigals who have never experienced true revival to ignite the fires of redemption in a nation which has strayed from the biblical principles of its forefathers? Young people must comprehend that their Christianity needs more than external events to survive.

What is it going to take to break out of this season of despair? What is the parent's role? the youth pastor's role? the teen's role? How did we get where we are? How did a bunch of on-fire parents in fervent, fiery churches end up with mediocre kids?

As I have traveled across America speaking to teenagers and their parents, I have reached this conclusion.

As the genuineness of our spiritual fire and commitment wanes, the chances for our youth to catch the fire diminish greatly.

God has given an incredible mandate to this generation, and we, as the older generation, must help them discover it. We must help them grasp the vision which will empower their lives. We must believe they have the potential to make a difference in their world.

In spite of apparent spiritual apathy, there are signs of a swelling revolution. We could be on the brink of an outpouring of God's grace on an entire generation throughout the world.

How can we be a catalyst for this movement in the lives of America's teens? How can we impact the youth in our homes and churches?

We stand on the threshold of opportunity. How will we respond? Will we answer destiny's knock at our door?

PART ONE

DESCRIBING THE CURRENT DILEMMA

Understanding — having it
causes wars to cease; lack of it can cause
divisions and grudges that last a lifetime. Most
of us spend a great deal of our time trying to get
others to understand us yet hardly any time
trying to understand others.
Understanding begins with a genuine desire
to find out what the other person is thinking
and feeling. As you read these first three chapters,
open up your heart to see life through the eyes
of a teenager, a parent and a youth leader.
Put yourself in their shoes. Try to imagine how
they feel. This could initiate the toppling of
barriers that have divided the generations
and prevented the passing of our passion for the
Lord to the younger generation.

ONE

THROUGH THE EYES OF A TEEN

JOHN SHUFFLES DOWN the hall toward the bathroom, buttoning his shirt as he goes. One glance at the huge hands of the grandfather clock tell him it's the final countdown of the weekly Sunday-morning drill.

"John, it's time to go to church!" his mother calls up the stairs. "Are you ready yet?"

"Oh, boy! My favorite time of the week," John mutters under his breath. Then he replies, "Yeah, Mom, just about ready."

Meanwhile he's thinking....

I guess it's good to have some spiritual input for the week. Nothing around here seems to have anything to do with what I hear about at church. I mean, we say the right words — "Praise the Lord" and "Hallelujah" — and pray every time before we eat. But the only time I hear the Bible is when it's used to convince me to do something I don't want to do. I hear a lot about God whenever there's a problem or when I'm doing something they don't like. But if I mention the fact that *they* don't act the way Pastor Fred says Christians ought to act, they say, "That is not the point."

The television is always on in my house — and not on Christian stations either. But when something comes on that I want to watch, we have to turn it to the Christian station. Mom and Dad and the whole family are so busy with jobs, activities, watching TV and reading the newspaper that they leave just enough time for us to shove God into our lives at church. The only time we get spiritual around our house is when the pastor comes over. Then Mom and Dad rush around the house hiding ashtrays, throwing away the last beer in the refrigerator, dusting off the Bible on the front table, turning off the TV, putting magazines away and making sure they put a Christian tape in the stereo just before he walks in.

It's not that I don't like God or that I don't want to be a Christian. Sometimes I just wonder what it really means to be a Christian. I've been going to church my whole life. I've been to youth group, and now I even go to a Christian school.

But if being a Christian means growing up in a dull environment, living a boring life and talking about long spiritual words all day, I don't know if I am into it.

Somehow I know there must be more. Mom put me into a Christian school because she didn't like the bad influences of public school. She thought I would have a whole new environment where everybody's a Christian and loves God. Right? Right!

On my first day of school, I was out in the parking lot, and I heard these guys talking about what was going on that weekend. There was just as much smoking and drinking and fooling around going on there as at my other school. But the art of secrecy had become a fine-tuned skill at the Christian school.

We go to Bible class every day and listen to our teacher talk about things we have heard a hundred times. There's never anything new — it's the same old stories and sermons. We have chapel at school a couple of times a week. They turn up the music so loud that you can't even hear yourself think. They try to get you excited about clapping and singing. It's not that I don't want to worship God — but I don't know how. It seems like such a stale and manufactured environment.

The people they get to speak at chapel usually act as if their message is the best news in the history of mankind. But most of the time I've already heard it. We used to get really great people to speak to us. But they never take into consideration anything that we think might be good for us. They'll have to do something really incredible to get my attention, because I'm not interested. I have more important things to think about, like what I'm doing after school today.

There are a few kids in my high school who really believe this stuff and act as if it's real. Everything they say is "Jesus this" and "Jesus that." They're fanatical. I don't know where they get their hype. They need to calm down and realize it's just the same old thing we've always heard.

Then there is the youth group. My mom makes me go every week. But my real friends are at my old school. They're the people I can really talk to and have a great time with. We're always playing some stupid mind game at the youth group meetings. Who belongs to what group, what guys are cool, or which girls are cute?

The youth pastor acts as if he has the newest, most exciting idea that ever hit the planet. But I'm thinking, I haven't had this much fun since I watched my brother's bedroom wall dry after we painted it.

I can't believe he actually expects us to stand up, clap our hands and sing. He expects all twenty of us to sing *loud* even though we don't know the words. I don't even want to know them. Besides, it has a lousy beat. I'm just trying to figure out if that girl who's been sitting next to me for the last couple of weeks really likes me or if she's just leading me on. A few weeks ago she tried to make Tom think she liked him. Before that, she liked Jeremy. But Tom said he likes this other girl.

The only reason Karen and Mike come is so they

can sneak out to an empty room and make out. And then there's that guy who wears the weird clothes and who nobody ever talks to. What a geek. Get a life. Get some real clothes. Open up your eyes.

This is supposed to be spiritual influence? I know my youth pastor means well, but I think he tries too hard. If he would just be himself, it would be a lot better.

I suppose that, in spite of all this, it's the right thing for me to go to church on Sunday. So I'll go. On the way to church everybody seems so spiritual. There's Christian music playing in the car. Dad and Mom are all dressed up. We rushed around the house at the last minute getting ready and getting everybody to the car. Luckily I didn't forget my Walkman. Good thing — now I'll have something constructive to do for the next couple hours of solid boredom. I figured out a way to put one of the ear plugs in my ear and cover it with my hair so that everybody thinks I'm paying attention. They haven't caught me yet. I just have to be careful how I run the cord up my shirt so that no one sees it.

Every week we have the same conversation when we get to church. Mom insists, "John, we want you to sit with us today."

So I beg. "Come on, Mom — let me sit in the back with all my friends."

"But you never want to sit with us," Dad says. "Are you too embarrassed to sit with us?"

"No, I just want to be with my friends."

Usually they give in and let me sit with my friends, who provide a little entertainment during the service. After all, I have a lot of gossip to get caught up on —

and to share. I count on those notes we pass back and forth every week to let me know what's going on.

The congregation shouts, "Jesus loves you!" and "Praise the Lord!" all morning long. It's not that I mind it, but it just seems so hollow and canned. When the music starts, I can't help wondering, Are we jamming or what? It sounds like something right out of the sixties or seventies — maybe even the forties. I'm sure my parents really like it. Yeah, we sang the same songs last week and the week before and the week before that. Yeah, right!

Now the leader is asking us to clap our hands — like any kid back here would clap his hands. But we humor them and sort of clap. I sure am getting excited now. Can you believe he's making us sing it again? "As the deer pants for water...." I wish that girl in front of me would comb her hair — she looks like a dog panting after getting stuck in a rainstorm. Maybe even a tornado!

Now it's getting really quiet because it's time for the pastor to preach. I wonder what he's going to say this week that I haven't heard before. Great, what does this guy mean? "The glory of God is filling this temple right now. His presence is infiltrating us so we will have the revelation of His omnipotence." I wish this guy would talk English. It's not that I don't want to listen, but when I can't understand a thing he says, how is it supposed to do me any good?

This whole Christian thing seems like an adult thing that they're just trying to con us kids into, especially when you hear stories like Jennifer's. Jennifer is sixteen years old, and she and her family have been in church all their lives. When Jennifer was five years old, her mom asked her if her dad had ever touched her in a way that scared her. Jennifer told her mom that he hadn't and asked why she wanted to know. Her mom said she had found a bunch of bad magazines that her dad had hidden and that she was afraid for Jennifer.

Since that day, Jennifer has never hugged her dad or said, "I love you." She was very cold to him because she was afraid of him. A year ago Jennifer's mom admitted that she was having an affair with a man from the Philippines. Although her mom says it's over, Jennifer isn't sure because the man keeps calling her mom on the phone. Jennifer used to feel called to be a missionary to the Asian people; now she hates every Oriental person she sees.

Her parents still go to church, lift their hands and worship God. Jennifer sits with them most of the time. They get mad at her when she doesn't lift her hands. It's no wonder she doesn't praise God since she's being forced to live a double life. Why would she want to follow her parents' example when their lives are so messed up?

If our parents would just do some of the stuff they tell us to do, it would be a lot easier. If the pastor made things relevant to where I am and what I'm going through, this Christianity stuff would probably be a whole lot easier to swallow.

TWO

THE
PARENT'S
PERSPECTIVE

DAD JINGLES THE car keys in his trouser pockets and grits his teeth, trying to keep a lid on his irritation. He watches John saunter across the upstairs landing, on his way back from the bathroom, then blurts out, "Come on, John — how many times do I have to tell you? It's time to leave — now!"

Every week it's the same struggle....

Why doesn't John like to go to church? Why do I have to tell him over and over again what time it starts and what he should wear and why he needs to go? The Lord led us to this church. I get so much out of the Word every week. The worship is incredible — all the songs are great. The pastor gives us fresh insights and revelation from the Word every week. I just don't know why John doesn't take interest.

I know it's hard being a teen these days with all the pressures they have to face. But when Jean and I got saved back in the sixties, the fire of God touched our hearts. I suppose some of the pressures are harder now than when we were growing up. We just want to keep John from having to go through the same weird things we had to experience. That's why we drag him to church and youth group every week. (Well, almost every week — unless something else comes up.)

We've given him everything he wants. We tried to do all the things we were supposed to do to make sure he was in the right environment. We even put him in a Christian school so he could be in a Christian atmosphere all the time. Of course, that took a big investment on our part, but we know it is worth it. He will get the good solid Christian foundation he needs.

I just don't understand why he doesn't like church. Why does he still want to listen to that rock music? You can't even understand the words. Why does he still want to hang around with those kids from his old school? They're just troublemakers. They say they don't get drunk or party, but I remember when I was a kid. I remember what they acted like and looked like.

Even though I hate to do it, sometimes I have to force him to come to church. I'm just trusting that the Word will give him the answers he needs as long as I keep him around it. Someday it will make sense to him. Why can't he just be as excited about God as I am or as I was when I first got saved? Why doesn't he act like a Christian? I've certainly been a good example for him. And why does he have to have that weird haircut?

Even the Christian music he listens to is wild and strange — I can't even tell it's Christian. You sure can't tell a Christian kid by the way they dress and do their hair. But I figure even if I have to force him to go to church, it's good for him to be in a spiritual environment. Sometimes I don't feel like lifting my hands or singing, but I do it to be a good example for John. Sometimes John catches me just looking around the room or writing a note during the sermon when he knows I should be paying attention. But I'm human too.

We've tried to do family devotions off and on through the years. We did them all the time when the kids were little — read them Bible stories and all. Sometimes you just get too busy with all the different things going on in your life. I know they've heard these stories and have them in their hearts. I know one thing — I can hang onto the Scripture verse that says, "Train a child in the way he should go, and when he is old he will not turn from it" (Prov. 22:6). He's almost grown now — sixteen years old — and I know he will not depart from the Christian walk.

I will stand in faith that what he has heard will come back to him. There is really not much I can do right now, except keep encouraging him to come to church.

I keep trying to talk to him about God whenever there's an opportunity. I tell him how he needs to obey his parents, read the Word and not watch so much TV. I am really busy myself. My wife and I used to spend a lot of time reading the Word together. But now we have soccer practice, cheerleading practice, work and church activities. It seems as if we're busy every night of the week. Our whole life is jammed full of things, and we haven't had much time to pray together. Lately I haven't even had time for my private devotions and prayer time.

I really didn't like it too much when John started wearing those clothes — black, wild-looking clothes with different kinds of silver gadgets. It seems as if that's what all the rebellious kids at school are wearing. But just because you wear a certain kind of clothes doesn't mean it has affected your heart. The most important thing is that he still believes in God, goes to church and wants to be a Christian. I'm sure all those other friends won't really affect him because he's been grounded in the Word for all these years.

I can't believe the youth pastor had the audacity to try to convince me he caught John with a cigarette at camp last summer. How could he possibly think I would believe him? I know my Johnny better than that. He would never get involved with cigarettes. If that kid would just get his heart right with God and get on his face, I know he would catch the same kind of revival I caught when I was about his age. Of course, if that youth pastor would shape up a bit, stop demanding that I do so much and start doing something himself, it would probably bring about a big change in John's life as well. Isn't that what we pay him for?

THREE

YOUTH PASTOR'S PERIL

PASTOR FRED PACES the front of the youth hall, his eyes eagerly scanning the rows of seats. It's finally Wednesday, and he can't wait for the meeting to start. Who knows? Maybe all the kids will show up tonight....

We're going to have a great time. God has been

speaking to my heart all week. I've put so much time into this, and I have visual aids and object lessons to use with my sermon. I sure hope *somebody* shows up, because I'm getting tired of begging them to come. I don't know where their priorities are. It seems as if every time there's something else going on at school — boom — it's the first thing they go to.

Like last year when I organized that sleep-over and pizza party, then found out the night before that there was a ball game that same night. No wonder only four or five of the whole group of twenty-five showed up. The ball game was just more important to them. I wish these kids would open their eyes and see what they really should be doing. Seems as if there is always something at school or some activity with their friends that conflicts with what God wants us to do here in the youth group.

Then there are the parents. I try my best to have a good youth program, but the parents never want to be involved. But they sure come running to me whenever there is a problem in their family. Then they want to talk and pray about it. But they won't bring their kids all week long to the different activities that are designed to help them. Of course, I can't get in their faces too much. What would the pastor say if they complained to him?

We definitely want to keep them coming to church. We don't want to offend them or anything. At the same time, someone's got to tell the parents that their kids are never going to change if they don't bring them consistently and get them involved.

Really, I love my teens. I know they love God. But why do they do the things they do?

Like Janet last week. She called me in the middle of the night when she was going through a tough time and wanted me to counsel her on the phone. And then the very next week she didn't show up at youth group. What's the deal? I spent my time trying to help her, but she only seems to need me when she is in trouble. I know what I should do. I should get really tough on them and make them sit up straight, take notes, keep their eyes open and stay awake. No. No. Maybe I should just love them and draw them in, hoping they will see Jesus in the love that I show them.

I hope these kids are ready for youth group this week. I really had to pray. I sure don't get any encouragement from them when I'm preaching. The looks on their faces when I open the Bible makes you think I'm asking them to drink spoiled milk. And I have to look at them — all those bored faces — for the next hour as I try to impart to them the things of God.

I've worked on my delivery to make it exciting and dynamic. Of course, sometimes I get loud and spit on them a little bit, but as long as they get the point my methods shouldn't matter much. No matter what I do they won't clap during worship or sing very loud — if at all. And no matter how much I ask them to witness in school or bring friends to the youth group, they don't do it.

Why aren't these kids budging? Why can't I get them to move forward in God? When I was a teenager I got excited about God. What's wrong with these kids? Why haven't they caught the same thing I caught when I was their age?

They don't seem to appreciate all that I do for them.

Why can't they see that I am only trying to help them? I want so badly for them to be able to stand against peer pressure and temptation. I preach about it, encourage them and give them object lessons; yet when the pressure is on they fall prey to it again.

I can see how tough it is being a teen these days. I want to help them. I seem to spend every waking hour helping these young people go through their struggles.

They have enormous needs — in their family life, at school, in dating relationships. Many of them have low self-esteem.

The temptations of drinking and drugs never seem to go away, and the high incidence of weapons being carried at school these days is putting fear in a whole generation of young people.

What can I do about all this? I am just one person in the midst of a barrage of complex problems for which I have no immediate answers. I must work harder to help as many as I can. I will keep planning more retreats, sleep-overs, fun nights, camps and other get-togethers to keep them busy. After all, if they get bored with youth group, they'll start looking for fun elsewhere — outside the church.

Where am I going to find the time to do more? I am already so stressed I can hardly function. I have almost no family life — my wife and children rarely see me anymore. I hope they understand that I'm doing it for the opportunity to reach these hurting teens. The day will come when I can spend more time with my own family. I hate having to miss my own kids' ball games and recitals, but what am I supposed to do?

Everyone seems to complain about how *the teens today are really messed up,* but they can't find the time to do something that will make a difference. I've tried so hard to get others at the church to help me, but to no avail. Why can't anyone else give up some time to help these kids?

I know my pastor has a heart for this broken generation. He's given me the freedom to do whatever I want. He's given me everything I ever asked for — except money. Not for me, but for youth ministry materials and activities. We just don't have a budget for the kind of stuff it takes to reach teens. I have some ideas that I am sure would make an incredible impact on the teens in our church and the whole community. However, with no cash available, there doesn't appear to be much opportunity to see it happen.

I feel such a passion to reach these teens, but it's an uphill battle. I have to convince the teens to come, convince the parents to bring them, convince the pastor to fund them and convince others in the church to work with me to help get the job done.

PART TWO

How We
Got Here

We are in a very
precarious situation with today's
teens. Frustration abounds from the teen's,
parent's and leader's perspectives. In spite
of our tendency to think we had no control
over teen issues, there are some
glaring realities that we must look at
if we are to find solutions.

FOUR

POST-REVIVAL PARENTS

As PARENTS WE find it hard to admit that our kids do not have the same zeal that we have (or had). How can it be that we who were swept off our feet in such an incredible revival could not communicate it to our own kids?

Let's take a look at the dynamics. Many of today's parents were part of the Jesus revolution of the late sixties and seventies. The Holy Spirit drew the spiritually down-and-out generation of the sixties into something that gave meaning and fulfillment to their lives. If you were a part of that movement, times of sitting around a campfire singing "Kum Ba Ya" and "Pass It On" are precious memories. Those were days filled with excitement and goose bumps — everyone was into Jesus. Prayer meetings lasted all night, and no one cared. People were devoted to reading the Word and having lengthy discussions about end times and other intriguing topics.

Whether or not you were saved during the Jesus movement, you can remember your own intense devotion during the early days of your salvation experience. It was like falling in love. Nothing else really mattered. You looked forward to prolonged worship times when you could get lost in the presence of God. You listened to hundreds of teaching tapes and went to hear every special speaker who came to town. You took notes eagerly during every sermon and attended any Bible study you could find.

Those were the signs of a passionate heart for God. Reading through the entire Bible was the most noble and diligent task you ever undertook. Older Christians probably even teased you for your zeal and told you that when you matured you would calm down. You were eager to witness to anything that moved. When faced with persecution from unsaved people around you, you just grew more committed.

It's exciting to reflect on our early days as Christians. Yet we would all agree that we must mature in the Lord. But what is spiritual maturity? What does it look like?

Accidental Stagnation

Although we can see through the immaturity of our earlier days, we would all say we still love God. But we can remember the embarrassing things we did *for the sake of Christ.*

The hard truth is, in the process of maturing we may have drifted a bit from our initial passion.

The evidence can be found in churches across America. Oh, people still raise their hands and sing to the Lord, but now they may be placing their focus on other people around them rather than on God. The shouts of "Hallelujah!" and "Praise the Lord!" sound somehow empty, lacking the thunder they once had. Note taking has dwindled into doodling because we've "already heard a sermon on that topic." Sharing our faith is still a priority, but we want people to see it in our lives — so we don't offend them with our words. "It will come up if God wants it to."

Songs that used to make us weep in the holy presence of God are now the "standard worship songs." Now that we have read the Bible through a time or two, it's not as important that we read it with the same diligence we once had.

These attitudes indicate a diminished passion for the deep things of God.

In some cases we have substituted knowledge for passion.

Spiritual Imitators

We assume we have learned all we can and have become content because we are so much more mature than we were in those early days. Most of our seeking of the Lord is a mere shadow of the earnest seeking we did in those earlier days.

The prophet Isaiah spoke of this spiritual lethargy:

> For day after day they seek me out; they *seem* eager to know my ways, as if they were a nation that does what is right and has not forsaken the commands of its God. They ask me for just decisions and seem eager for God to come near them (Is. 58:2, italics added).

We often do the thing that would bring us close to God, but we do it without the passion of someone who is earnestly seeking intimate fellowship with Him. The people of Isaiah's day attempted to draw close to God through a fast.

> "Why have we fasted," they say, "and you have not seen it? Why have we humbled ourselves, and you have not noticed?" (Is. 58:3).

Just like the fast Isaiah describes, we go through the motions but have forgotten the meaning behind them.

What Are We Communicating?

In the midst of all this, we try to communicate to our young people the importance of loving God. Most of what we share with them is a reflection of what we had while we were in our early days in Christ. Our desire to impart what we received from God is noble, but our frustration level grows when we fail to see the fruit we had hoped for in their lives.

I have seen many casualties of this kind of pseudo-fiery Christianity. Some young people, watching the fake hype over a period of time, begin to imitate it. They long for the real thing but have only seen the imitation.

In one of our services a fourteen-year-old boy came forward for prayer. I watched him peek out of one eye to see if I was watching him worship. As we prayed for him he kept repeating, "O Lord, please make me shake."

Another sixteen-year-old young woman who had traveled overseas with Teen Mania had a habit of "falling out under the Spirit" at any moment she chose. Our leaders knew she was doing it for attention and were trying diplomatically to help her mature. One day she "went down" as the team was going to a school to minister. The leader sent the rest of the team on and stayed behind to help her up. Later some of the other teens saw her dragging her leg and asked why. She replied, "My leg is still out under the Spirit." This sounds comical, but it is a sad commentary on what has been modeled for our young people.

Physical Growth Without Spiritual Growth

These kids did great when they were younger children. They were involved in Sunday school and children's church; they memorized Scripture verses, asked questions about the Lord and prayed eagerly for people who were sick or hurting. We can remember their creative attempts at sharing their faith with their peers and others and recall that they were "so cute."

But now that these children have become teens, things have really changed. As a parent who sincerely loves God, you attend a church that encourages your spiritual growth through fellowship and teaching. Yet your teen sits there next to you in the pew and seems to get nothing out of the services. You know he is bored, but you do not know what to do.

You try to talk him into being interested; you offer him rewards or even force him to go. It's hard for you to understand *why* he does not want the same kind of relationship with Jesus that you have.

You believe that taking him to youth group should fix his problem. After all, you didn't have a progressive youth program when you were growing up, and yet you managed to grow spiritually. Your busy-ness increases as you take him to every youth activity, hoping that something will break through to him. Finally you observe a bit of a breakthrough upon his return from a retreat, only to watch it wane after a few weeks. You wonder, Whatever happened to the kind of commitment we had when we were young?

Putting on the Pressure

You resort to forced spiritual discussions with your teenager, using the words and rhetoric that have always pushed your spiritual hot buttons. "Praise the Lord for His glory filling our lives!" you shout with excitement. But your teen stares at you with a blank expression.

These dated spiritual expressions sound like meaningless spiritual gibberish to most teens. Sharing the stories of what happened to you when you were young is ineffective — they have heard them many times before. "I remember when I was your age. I was all messed up in drinking, and the Lord set me on fire!" you say as the memory of that experience floods you with emotions. But your teen turned off as soon as you said, "I remember...."

He is thinking, So you went out and had your fun first, but you don't want me to have mine? or, Why are you telling me this again? Do you think I didn't hear you the first hundred times you told the story? Your sharing becomes a lecture about all sorts of theology and other issues that appear to be completely irrelevant to his life. Harping on habits that he holds dear seems to be your last-ditch effort to keep him from ruining his life.

The root of your frustration lies in the fact that you have done all you were told to do to have a godly child. You have lived a good life, kept your children in church and maybe even put them in a Christian school. Now what do you do?

At this point many parents just hold on to the promise, "Train a child in the way he should go, and when he is old he will not turn from it" (Prov. 22:6).

It is not enough to have the fire yourself. If it is real, why can't we pass it on to the next generation?

It is not enough to expect them merely to mimic your spiritual fervor.

We must somehow discover how to transmit it to the next generation in a way that does not push them away from us but leads them to the loving God whom we ourselves follow. The Bible says, "Each heart knows its own bitterness, and no one else can share its joy" (Prov. 14:10).

Because we desire to see our kids on fire for God, we resort to tactics that none of us would have responded to ourselves. We must discover the ingredients in our lives that made our excitement possible — as they will for our teens. Everyone knows that to start a fire and keep it going you must have wood, paper, kindling, gasoline and matches. As we identify the ingredients of the fire burning in our own lives, we can provide these basic ingredients to our kids to start their own spiritual fire.

We can impact this next generation with strategy, conviction and consistency.

FIVE

THE
BREAKDOWN OF
RELATIONSHIPS

THE FRAGMENTED, DISJOINTED lifestyle of the average American family does not lend itself to wholesome and productive family relationships. Think about it — the pace of living has increased in every arena of life during the past few decades.

American Family Life

First let's look at Dad — busy trying to make a living and provide for his family so that their needs are met and they can taste a little of the "good life" that America promises. This drives him to work overtime in the office and accounts for his preoccupation with work when he is home.

Next, in order to be well-rounded, the kids are encouraged to be involved in sports, clubs, dancing lessons, spelling bees, boy scouts and girl scouts, church activities, music lessons and fund-raising events. Each of these commitments brings a ritual of activities which must be fulfilled to succeed. As a result, life becomes a flurry of scheduled busy-ness for the kids.

Mom is caught in the midst of this flurry. The responsibility of being family activities coordinator consumes her life. She must take Johnny to soccer practice; make sure Susie has a ride home from cheerleading on the right days of the week; chauffeur everyone to all their scheduled activities; and still fulfill her household responsibilities of shopping, cooking, cleaning and budgeting. Besides all this, she must try to find personal time to be alone. In addition, many of today's mothers work outside the home, and for these women the daily schedule becomes an exercise in frustration and dread.

Today's family spends very little time together. We feel fortunate when we can catch a meal around the table together once in a while. We have our own lives, our own schedules of busy-ness, and our own goals and passions into which we are pouring ourselves. Most of our communication has to do with information about these busy schedules we keep instead of about the persons keeping the schedules. We're buzzing around all over the city all day and come home only to eat, sleep and get ready for the next day.

The home has become a hotel for relatives rather than a haven to foster relationships and grow with each other through life.

We sit around the table and talk to people we really do not even know. We eat with family members who in reality are strangers to us. How much do we know about what is really going on in their lives? What are they thinking? What are they feeling? How are they hurting? What challenges are they facing?

We sleep under the same roof with people we hardly know. Our homes are filled with people who are desperately lonely and feel no one wants to listen to them.

For many teenagers, depression peaks in the latter half of the teen years. Two to four times more teenagers are depressed than are middle-aged people, and up to seven times more teenagers are depressed than people sixty-five and older.[1] People in our own homes may be crying themselves to sleep every night without our even being aware of it.

The Price the Family Has Paid

This lifestyle has taken its toll on this generation of families and on the young people they are rearing. Over one million children are seeing their parents separate every year, and more than one-fourth of the households in the United States are single-parent families.[2]

The average length of a marriage in the United States is seven years, according to the 1990 census. Studies show that the average father interacts with his baby for less than thirty-eight seconds a day.[3] Edwin Louis Cole states that the average American father gives only "thirty-five seconds of undivided attention to his child each day."[4]

Of the time we do spend at home, most of it is spent following individual pursuits. For example, 72 percent of families watch television every day, and 35 percent are "total TV households," meaning that their TVs are turned on all afternoon, at dinnertime and all evening.[5]

This serves to deepen the isolation that each family member feels. Psychologists have found that extended television watching intensifies the loneliness family members feel.[6]

Much of the time that teens spend at home is spent alone in their rooms. Some 28 percent own their own phone, and 47 percent own their own television.[7] More than 80 percent of sixth- to ninth-graders said their top afternoon activity is watching television. In fact, some researchers note that one of the only things that teenagers have in common these days, whether rich or poor, is access to a TV, a VCR and a Walkman.[8]

Yet these communication devices have served to isolate them even more.

It is not uncommon for a teen to hang a "Do not disturb" sign on his door in the name of privacy and to retreat to a world of high-tech toys and isolation.

One study indicated that during the period between

ten and fifteen years of age, the amount of time a young person spends with his family decreases by one half.[9] Beatrix Hamburg, director of child and adolescent psychology at New York's Mount Sinai School of Medicine, says that "teenagers are spending a lot of time alone in their rooms."[10]

A Changing Culture

Some of the isolation is due to a cultural change. There seems to be an age segregation in the kind of activities that teens and families like to do together.[11] In place of family outings and vacations, entertainment is geared toward age groupings.

For example, going to certain kinds of "teen movies" or frequenting teen hangouts drives teenagers away from family fun together.[12] Even the types of jobs available to young people push them into their own peer group rather than toward the family. Fast-food chains, for example, typically hire teens and thus make family time less feasible.

Home Alone

Because of the many homes where both parents work, many children are "latchkey kids." These teens go home to an empty house where 16 percent make their own dinner and 11 percent cook for other family members.[13]

As a result, we have a runaway problem in America like never before — about 1.5 million kids run away each year. Most have this in common: They think their parents have no interest in them.[14] Almost all of the runaways are teenagers, and a disproportionate number of these are from stepfamilies.[15]

Many stepparents do not consider their stepchildren a part of their "close family."[16] Half of the children in the United States will experience the breakup of their parents' marriage, and one in ten will suffer through three divorces.[17]

Changing Parental Attitudes

In 1980, of the parents surveyed in America, 75 percent felt they should be free to live their own lives even if it meant spending less time with their children.[18] In another study two out of three men said they would likely take a job for money or prestige even if it took more time away from their families. This is in spite of their expressed desire for more family time.[19]

Emotional Pain Results

In addition, we find that one out of three adult women and one out of seven adult men were sexually abused before the age of eighteen. The particularly frightening part of this is that research has indicated that 29 percent of those women were first abused by their biological fathers.[20] It is no wonder that two out of every ten young people are moderately to severely depressed.[21] Other studies have shown that ten percent of boys and twenty percent of girls have attempted suicide.[22]

The traditional family is a real minority in America.

The decade of the nineties is not friendly to a lifestyle that cultivates healthy family relationships.

The Price Teens Have Paid

All this busy-ness has taken its toll on today's youth. We wonder why our teens seem unwilling to listen to us, but all they see is a lifestyle of confusion and fragmentation. Their stability has been yanked out from underneath them, and there is no one to talk to about it. Who is listening to the hurts of this broken-hearted generation?

If parents will not listen to their teenagers, then those teens are forced to find someone who will listen. Sometimes it may be a caring relative, but more often it is an acquaintance at school who has been through the same thing. One survey showed that 58 percent of high schoolers would be more likely to seek advice from a peer than an adult.[23] They are more likely to consider their friends a greater influence on them than their parents.[24] Together they build each other's cynicism of the older generation as they construct a lifestyle of rebellion.

As a result, only 22 percent of sixteen- and seventeen-year-olds report that they gained most of their knowledge about sex from their parents. A whopping 70 percent attribute their knowledge of sex to friends, school and entertainment.[25]

MTV says it listens to its listeners and credits that as the reason for its success.[26] Letters from viewers say things like, "No one else even pretends to care about what we think," or "I have a question, and I figured that if anyone could help me you guys could." Many of the letters are signed with statements saying, "Sincerely with much devotion and love." No wonder this music network touts itself as a trusted adviser that understands and respects teens. MTV is giving advice to this generation.

Is it not a sad commentary on our parenting that today's youth find MTV, a medium driven by high-paying sponsors, more willing to listen than we, their parents, who are supposedly driven by love for them?

These feelings of estrangement have not escaped the young people in the church. As I travel across America, I see that the residue of this lifestyle has tarnished the hope and wholeness of today's young people who have been raised in the church.

My wife and I went to visit one sixteen-year-old young man who had sat down on his front lawn, poured gasoline on himself and set himself on fire. It was a miracle he even lived, with 96 percent of his body burned. He had no eyelids, no ears, no nose or lips. He hardly looked human. Half of his arm had burned off, and he could no longer walk.

"Mark, what in the world would make you want to end your life like this?" I asked.

Mark responded the best he could with no lips: "When I was a kid, my parents got a divorce. I don't know — I guess I never got over it."

Mark had been reared in church; his parents had gone to church, and his stepparents had gone to church. Yet he felt he had no one to talk to. How many others like Mark sit in our youth groups and at our dinner tables across America? After a tragic family split, the world tells us, "They will get over it." But they are not getting over it — at least not without specific efforts targeted to minister directly to this need.

I hear story after story as I preach to thousands of teens each week. They say things like, "I cannot remember the last time my parents told me they loved me." This in spite of the fact that these kids have been raised in a home where the parents love God and go to church regularly.

I remember sobs from teenage young men as we prayed over those who felt as if they were abandoned by their fathers. Those who still had fathers present in their homes felt the same abandonment as those with absent fathers, since their fathers never talked to them. Their only desire is to have a father to look up to and talk to, and their only hope is the promise that God will be "a father to the fatherless" (Ps. 68:5). This has not happened just one time — countless times across this nation auditoriums have been flooded by the tears of today's teens.

A Generation of Broken Hearts

The stories of teenagers that I have included in this book are not made up — nor are they uncommon. We have polled thousands of teens across America who have been raised in church to find out what they are thinking and feeling. One question was, "What one thing would you tell your parents if you knew you would not get in trouble for it?" Among the most common responses were:

- I'd like to be closer.

- Quit comparing me to my sisters.

- I love you, and I wish you would listen to my side of the story for once.

- How you make me feel when you cut me down.

- Why do you always think you are right and I am wrong?

- Why don't you ever talk to me about personal things?

- I wish you could tell me more often that you love me.

- I hate my life.

- I hate my half sister getting all the attention.

- I am having premarital sex.

- Please understand me.

- You're a bunch of hypocrites.

- I would tell my father he is an alcoholic jerk who makes me feel like a nothing.

- I wish you would stop fighting because I can't take it anymore.

- I love you, and thanks for being there.

- Sometimes you hurt me terribly.

- You need to understand this generation and this culture.

- Why do you always make promises that you don't keep?

- Why can't you forget about past mistakes?

- Give me the respect of trusting me.

- I'm not perfect and don't always think of the right thing to do.

- Please listen to me when I have a problem, and if I'm in trouble, ask me if I need help.

We also asked them, "What feelings have you tried to communicate that your parents just do not understand?" These are some of their responses:

- I'm lonely.

- Being a teen is harder than it appears.

- I hurt.

- I sometimes feel you don't love me.

- I don't like myself (low self-esteem).

- Life is very difficult.

- I don't understand love.

- I'm older than you treat me.

- I have tried to communicate too many feelings to list.

- I want to be accepted, and if you don't accept me I'll go nuts.

- I was hurt during the divorce.

- I feel guilty, and I don't know what to do about it.

- I'm angry.

- I often need to do things my way, even if it seems wrong to you. Just let me learn from it.

- I'm trustworthy if you would just listen.

- I want to be sort of independent and to be trusted.

- I never know how to say things that I want.

- I am depressed and confused.

When asked, "What would be the first thing you would change if you were in charge of your family?" the two most common responses were, "I would improve the communication" and "I would schedule a regular family devotional time."

The older generation must stop long enough to listen to what our teenagers are saying.

Though we attempt to influence them with our values and our Lord, their vision is distorted by a relationship vacuum.

It's like a stranger giving advice.

If we want to influence this generation, we must go the extra mile to understand them and re-establish a relationship with them. If we want them to listen to us, we must listen to them first.

SIX

NOTHING
TO DIE
FOR

WHEN I WAS growing up, I wanted to be a lawyer or a doctor. I was told I had college potential and that by all means I should pursue it. Even though no one in my family had ever been to college before, I knew that by virtue of living in the United States of America I could do whatever I wanted to do.

Most of us grew up with a sense of desire and hope for

the future. We dreamed of being a fireman, an astronaut or the president. We were told we could be whatever we wanted to be if we worked hard enough for it.

Many of us were told that going to college would be our key to success. The American dream seemed attainable for all and was a noble cause for which to pour out our lives. Our ability to dream was the only thing that would limit us — so we were told. For most of us, our career became our quest in life — something to be pursued and conquered.

The Legacy of Each Decade

Each of the past several decades has had a distinguishing mark which served to identify "the cause" for that generation's young people. In the midst of striving to find their piece of the American dream, each generation has emerged with an identity that marks them and becomes part of their heritage as they move into adulthood.

When we remember the fifties, our minds rehearse reruns of "Happy Days." But however happy those days seem, they were not without struggle. This was the first generation of American teenagers to identify themselves as distinctly different from adults and children. Before the fifties, children sort of evolved into adulthood, as John Boy did in "The Waltons." But during the fifties the rise of rock 'n' roll music became the anthem of a newly emerging subculture called *teenagers*. Rebellion against their parents' standards was the battle cry from their cigarette-smoking lips and could be seen in their beer-can-raised fists.

The sixties were marked by the same rebellion but

with a different expression. These young extremists rallied behind the anti-war movement, which became a uniting force for teenagers nationwide. Anti-war slogans soon turned into an anti-establishment war cry. Anything run by the older generation was a threat to the real freedom for which the youth of the day cried out. The "anti" sentiment soon turned into an anti-American dream. Youth despised the success achieved by gaining social status, following career tracks and accumulating material possessions.

Nevertheless, these principled youth began to blend into the very establishment against which they fought as they took the responsibilities of life and child rearing seriously. Many of the Yuppies (young urban professionals) of the eighties were the anti-establishment young people from the sixties.

The disillusionment of the sixties, which initiated drug use as a part of the teen subculture, became the launching pad of a whole decade of drug abuse in the seventies. Even though the Vietnam War had ended for America in the early seventies, distrust of the older generation continued throughout the decade. Many refused to pursue the careers that would put them right in the middle of the system they so mistrusted. "Do what you want to do" and "If it feels good — do it" were the anthems of the day.

The eighties emerged with a whole new belief in the American system during the Reagan years. A sense of hope and patriotism had been restored. The economy boomed after the devastation of the oil recession. Pursuing the American dream seemed to be the right thing to do. Live life with gusto.

Living on credit cards to afford an extravagant lifestyle became the norm. The energy of the young generation was poured into education and long-term planning for the future. They would not be duped by the same thing that stole the future from the previous decade. As they pursued all the things that America promised, designer drug use crept into the lifestyles of the young people.

The Nineties' Legacy-less Generation X

Today we have a generation of young people who lack the zest to pour their lives into anything. Although the residue of each of the previous generations is evident in the young people of the nineties, there seems to be no battle cry.

This listlessness is due in part to the breakdown in the family. This is the first generation of latchkey kids — 50 percent of whom were raised in homes divided by divorce — to emerge into adulthood. Or, as one writer put it, "they have virtually reared themselves, while the TV provided some surrogate parenting."[1]

Their future appears far dimmer than that of past generations. Many young people believe they will have a harder time accomplishing the same standard of living that their parents have.[2] They believe their counterparts partied through the seventies and eighties and left them with the bill — the national debt.

As a result, many people are calling this group of young people "Generation X." They have no distinguishing characteristic — hence the "X." This group of young Americans ranges in age from early teens to mid-twenties. They fall between the famous baby boomers and the children of the baby boomers. They arrived on the scene as a miracle, since the wide-spread use of contraception methods, such as the pill, had just begun and abortion had just been legalized. Because they are a smaller group, especially compared to the boomers, they are largely an unsung generation. Except for the trouble they get into, they are barely noticed at all.

Time magazine describes them this way:

> They have trouble making decisions. They would rather hike the Himalayas than climb the corporate ladder. They have few heroes, no anthems, no style to call their own. They crave entertainment, but their attention span is as short as the zap of a TV dial. They hate Yuppies, hippies and druggies. They postpone marriage because they dread divorce. They possess only a hazy sense of their own identity but a monumental preoccupation with all the problems the preceding generation will leave them to fix.[3]

They have no cause for which to stand. As a generation, they have no battle cry. They have no distinctive clothes, sports or activities — nothing stands out. The music of the day is either a remake of tunes from previous decades or the grunge rock which sounds like a lot of noise, buzz and angry lyrics.[4] In fact, during the writing of this manuscript Kurt Cobain, the lead singer of Nirvana (often referred to as the spokesmen for Generation X), with songs that writhe in helplessness, shot and killed himself.

The dress for this aimless group contrasts with the

image of money. It defers to the grunge look of sloppy flannel shirts worn untucked, sloppy hair and tattered jeans.

> *Virtually every area of their lives is expressly undefined — as undefined as their own definition of who they are.*

Even the secular media is noting the lack of motivation among today's teens and young adults as they launch into their post-college careers only to find what is called a "McJob." These mundane and marginally challenging jobs supply money on which to survive but not much else. Only one in five college graduates has a job requiring a degree.[5]

Current Events Shaping the Day

When surveying the current events that have shaped our young people, it is easy to see why they have a disdain for their future. When the older generation is asked to name the one event that defines their upbringing, they might respond, "the bombing of Pearl Harbor" or "the assassination of President Kennedy." Today's generation remembers the space shuttle Challenger exploding. They remember their teacher breaking down and crying as he or she mourned a colleague. As Arthur Levine has noted, "Beyond the fact that it was the first generational tragedy, students talked of a shattering of their idealism and their sense of safety."[6]

The end of the cold war is also a part of their

heritage. However exciting it was for the rest of the world, a lurking anxiety popped up in the younger generation. At least you knew who your enemy was with the cold war on. Now it could be anyone. Ironically, the end of the cold war seemed to bring less security.

The Persian Gulf War, while first inspiring patriotism, has had a negative effect on some. The strong, decisive victory of the United States was great, but thoughts linger in the minds of young people: It's still a mess. Why didn't we finish the job? Was it politically motivated?[7]

Combine these issues with the AIDS epidemic and the Rodney King racial upheaval, and it's easy to see why today's youth are less defined on who they are and where they are going. It is no wonder that suicide rates among teens have tripled since 1950 and that suicide is the third leading cause of death among young people fifteen to twenty-four years old.[8] As a result we have a generation that does not know why it is here, nor does it have much motivation to make the discovery.

Where Does the Church Fit in This?

The lack of purpose in this generation of young people is at epidemic proportions, and the church has not done much to alleviate the problem. Most youth groups are seen as peripheral to the main needs of the church. Parents consider it an inconvenience to take teens to youth activities, yet they often go to great lengths to keep them involved in school activities. We parents want our teens to be committed to the Lord, but not so much that they embarrass us in public.

Comfortable Christianity Without a Cause

For so long the Christianity teens have seen has catered to their comforts and conveniences instead of demanding their all. How many times have you heard a statement similar to this during an altar call: "If you want to be a Christian, all you have to do is..."? What do we mean by "all you have to do"? According to Jesus, all you have to do is hate your mother and father (Luke 14:26); lay down your life (Luke 9:24); put your hand to the plow and don't look back (Luke 9:62); let the dead bury their own dead (Luke 9:60); eat His flesh and drink His blood (John 6:53); and take up your cross and follow Him (Matt. 10:38). That's all! He demands our all.

God knows you are made out of the stuff that desires to give its all to something.

That is why He says:

> Whatever you do, work at it with all your heart (Col. 3:23).

Jesus challenged His disciples to the core of who they were. He wants everyone to come to Him — but only on His conditions. We say we would die for Him; but then it rains, and we don't want to go to church because we might get our hair messed up. The package of Christianity that we have given this young generation lacks the substance that dares them to sink their teeth into it and never let go.

*Until you find a cause worth dying
for, you are not really living.*

This is even the problem of young people who have
been raised in exciting church environments. They
have been around it all their lives yet do not realize it
is the *only* thing worth giving their lives for.

The football coach never apologizes for telling his
guys to push harder. He inspires them with a reason
to give their all. They are defending the reputation of
the school and represent the entire student body.
They must do *whatever it takes* to win the championship. Do we have less to live for than the local football
team? We are defending the name of the awesome
creator God. We represent the holy Son of God who
gave His life for us all.

*Many of us have forgotten why we
were trying to get our kids to go to
church in the first place.*

The goal shifted from the end result to the process
of getting them there — where we hope they like it or
don't complain too much. As a result we have a generation of churched kids who are just as purposeless
as their unsaved peers. They are just as disillusioned
with the church as the heathens are with society in
general. The parents found the excitement and now
expect the teens to find the same thing without the
calling and conviction that brought the parents in the
first place.

The church-wise teenagers who fill our churches

and youth groups across the country are a product of the brand of Christianity that begs people to keep coming back to church. When "many of His disciples went back and walked with Him no more" (John 6:66, NKJV), Jesus confronted His trusted twelve disciples by asking, "Do you also want to go away?" (John 6:67, NKJV). He was constantly trying to get rid of people who were not willing to give it their all.

Most Americans think they are doing God a favor by going to church. As a result Christianity is perceived as a social activity rather than something for which to die. They are more willing to give their all for the coach than for the King of kings.

This generation is waiting for the challenge that will demand their all. They are waiting to find something to pour their lives into — something to sink their teeth into. They have become disillusioned with both the secular world and the Christian world. Our greatest natural resources — the vision and energy of a whole generation of youth — are being squandered. We must show them a Christianity that will answer their cry for a meaningful life.

It is time to call them to give their lives away for a cause greater than themselves. We need to let them know there is a Christ to live for and a cause worth dying for. The cause is to give our lives for the One who gave His life for us. Let's transform Generation X into a generation that stands for the *cross*.

SEVEN

COMPETING WITH THE RAZZLE-DAZZLE OF THE WORLD

WITH THE UPROAR of worldly voices competing for the attention of our teens, it is easy to see why we might feel compelled to employ their tactics.

MTV brags about its ability to influence the "MTV generation" as it flaunts its role in increasing the voter turnout of young adults by 20 percent in the 1992 election. It proudly states that it is one of the few entities that listen to this generation and give them what they want.[1]

In addition, all the ads, magazines, TV shows and live concerts bombarding the senses of our youth seem to outdo anything we as Christians can put together to communicate with them. More recently, Nintendo and Sega games have captured the attention of these young ones with interactive games that place you in the middle of the video action, stealing creativity and initiative from our youth.

Studies have shown that by the time a teen graduates from high school he has watched more than eighteen thousand hours of television. That is six thousand more hours than he is spending in the classroom.[2]

The media have kidnapped our kids right from under our noses, and we don't even know it.

How should we respond to this kind of media bombardment?

Many parents do not respond at all. They just keep bringing their kids to youth group and hope that everything will be all right.

Some churches have tried their best to imitate the hype the world uses. They turn the music up loud, use *cool* words at youth group meetings and try to make Christianity look like just as much fun as the world.

In youth groups across America you will find all kinds of Christian versions of "pin-the-tail-on-the-donkey" and "romper room." The teens sit in the back and roll their eyes at the youth leader, who thinks he is the epitome of relatability with his silly outfit and worldly antics.

A lot of money is spent on the production of up-to-date, innovative ideas for teaching Christian kids. Don't get me wrong — I am all for having a great time and relating to teens with a medium that shows we understand how they learn.

Jesus was a master at relating to His audiences in a way they could understand. To the fishermen He talked about fishing, and to the farmers He talked about planting seed. He used lilies and sparrows as object lessons to get His point across.

How should we respond to this kind of media bombardment?

The important distinction is that your creativity is driven by the message you want to communicate — not the competition from the world.

We don't have to try to be better than the world; the world could never equal what we have in Christ. We don't have to hype it up and dress it up to make it seem better than it is. Our challenge is to present it in such a way that they see *what* it is that God has.

At Teen Mania's Acquire the Fire conventions across North America, we use a live band, light show, live drama, large-screen video walls and more to communicate to the teens. At different times controlled pyrotechnic explosions may go off to emphasize a memory verse, or a video roll-in may appear on the monster video screens to reiterate a point being made. Our intention is to use the media of the world *to communicate,* because that's the way teens listen. We are *not* trying to imitate what the world does.

One trip to a modern secular rock 'n' roll concert will prove to you that we truly cannot compete. Even with all the equipment we use at the Acquire the Fire conventions, we as a ministry cannot compete.

Jesus did not die so that we could run a race against the world to see who is the coolest.

We will lose if we try to compete, and the teens will see us and the gospel we are trying to communicate as foolish. They will think, This is just a second-rate version of what real fun is like.

Parents and youth leaders find themselves in this trap. Trying to attract kids with a myriad of "fun" activities is not enough. We will think we have done our job because we have kept the kids sheltered in a Christian environment or because they keep coming back. As we search desperately for fun things to do, we hope they don't discover that the world may be having a lot more fun than they are. We plan camps, bake sales, ball teams, sing-alongs, concerts, conferences and other youth fun times, but the void remains.

Many youth pastors have experienced the frustration of working extremely hard to put one of these events together. The youth pastor makes the flyers, puts up the posters, does the mailings, makes the announcements and begs the kids to come. He does the fund raisers, gets more volunteers, announces it to the parents and puts it in the church bulletin. He makes a huge placard or mural in the youth room to remind the teens of the event and hypes the publicity in anticipation of the event. Then he discovers that all but two members of his youth group went to the ball game being held on the same night. He reaps no benefit for all his hard work.

Jesus did not die so that we could have good clean fun. A lot of non-Christians have good clean fun too. Is that the goal of our time spent with our young people? What *is* our goal?

We have become satisfied with a maintenance mode of Christianity. As long as we maintain the status quo, we are doing OK. Parents are satisfied that, as long as the youth group is not getting into trouble, the church must be doing a good job. Well-meaning youth pastors and parents are plagued by this mentality, but the fact that they are not seeing any real fervor in their kids' lives escapes their focus.

First Timothy 4:12 says, "Don't let anyone look down on you because you are young." Yet so many adults despise the youthful Christianity we see around us. We are never sure if we can take seriously a young person who calls himself a Christian — especially if you find one who is really excited, because you wonder what he will be excited about *next* week.

The Christianity of our young people seems to be based so much on events and feelings. I have seen unsaved teens leave secular concerts with the same kind of hype-euphoria that Christian teens have after a Christian event. Losing their commitment to the Lord is likened to losing their commitment to a band. What is so bad about that? Don't we want them to be excited? This is what many think, of course. So we keep arranging entertaining Christian events. Inadvertently we are encouraging this roller-coaster Christianity by fueling their desire for these events.

Let me say once again that events themselves are not bad. But we must know the purpose that drives the events. God planned many special feasts and holidays, all with a purpose. If your vision for your youth group or teen inspires the purpose for your events, then you are not doing them to compete with the world, and your kids' stability does not lie in your activity but in the purpose behind it. But this is the reality:

Most of our activities have nothing to do with our purpose as Christians in this world.

We want our teens to be excited about Jesus so we plan events that will help fuel their excitement. But the Bible *never commands us to be excited about Jesus*. In fact, the word *excitement* is never used in the Bible (NIV).

But the Scripture talks a lot about commitment and fervor for the Lord. When we go after excitement, it's like chasing the wind — you grab for it but never catch it. Hence we keep going after another experience hoping it will be the thing that will really keep our teenagers fired up.

We need to make sure our attention is directed on building a relationship with Jesus Christ. If you seek intimacy with Him, He will keep your fire going. When all the crowd is gone, you cannot hold on to excitement. You cannot count on the thrill staying with you. But if you reach out and grab commitment, you can take that with you wherever you go. You can hold on to your commitment whether a crowd of excited teens is there cheering you on or not.

We need to transform this generation of Christians into those who are not slaves to how they feel but are governed by the commitments they make.

The razzle-dazzle of the world won't keep our teens fired up. Purpose, commitment, identity and a sense of belonging to something much greater than this world are the only things that will maintain the teens' fervor.

We do not have to compete with the world. We do not have to dress up the gospel. We just need to impart its power. We do not need fake hype — we have the Inventor of the only real excitement there is. We were not created to be motivated by outward stimuli. No matter how much you cram into your five senses, it will never be enough to sustain your desire. That is why drugs, alcohol and sex don't satisfy — you are craving something inside.

We were designed to be stimulated inwardly by the presence of the living God. The anointing of His presence will blow away any gimmick the world tries to use to attract attention. That is what Simon the sorcerer tried to buy after he recognized its appeal over the magic he had practiced for so long (see Acts 8:9-24). He had never seen the real thing before, but he knew he wanted it.

Our teens need the real thing — an encounter with the living God. Once you give them the real thing they will never want the fake stuff again.

PART THREE

CHANGING OUR PERSPECTIVE

Sometimes our perception varies
significantly from someone else's view of the same
thing. Those involved in law enforcement practice the
art of eliminating perceptual differences in people's
outlook of the same crime. The way we respond
to a person or situation is dictated by how we
perceive the circumstances.
We have examined this generation through the eyes
of modern fact finders, sociologists and journalists.
For most of us, the media dictate our perspective. We
have looked at their view of this generation of youth.
Now let us examine another perspective.
How does God see them?
Our natural instinct is to feel a little sorry for
them and just hope for the best. When one excels,
we patronize him. Our perception of their
circumstances hinders us from giving them the
respect they deserve.
It is time to discard the outlook that has been
systematically shoved down our throats as the truth
about today's teenagers. As we look at God's view we
must open our hearts to change and treat them as
God does. As we change our thinking about this
generation, a new hope and excitement will rise
as we witness the spiritual revolution about
to break forth through teenagers.

EIGHT

How Does God See This Generation?

IN THE MIDST of a negative worldview about today's young people it is easy to give up hope. The front page of newspapers and the television lead-ins are overcrowded with statistics such as those we quoted in previous chapters of this book.

How many times must we hear things like "This generation has the worst SAT scores since the beginning of mankind" before we start to believe that *all* teens are dumb? We have been blitzed with so many drug overdose stories that they do not carry much impact anymore.

Now as we hear about a purposeless "Generation X" it can make us feel paralyzed: What can I do that would really make a difference? Many people resolve simply to "watch and see" how it will all turn out in the end.

Seeing Beyond the Obvious

In Matthew 16:2-3 Jesus said, "When evening comes, you say, 'It will be fair weather, for the sky is red,' and in the morning, 'Today it will be stormy, for the sky is red and overcast.' You know how to interpret the appearance of the sky, but you cannot interpret the signs of the times."

He explains again in Luke 12:54, "When you see a cloud rising in the west, immediately you say, 'It's going to rain,' and it does. And when the south wind blows, you say, 'It's going to be hot,' and it is. Hypocrites! You know how to interpret the appearance of the earth and sky. How is it you do not know how to interpret this present time?"

Jesus was commenting on their lack of ability to see what was going on around them and make plans for the future. They seemed to be experts on the physical things that predicted the weather but completely ignorant about the spiritual signs all around them. There they were, making all kinds of fuss about rules, regulations and the wind.

They had the Son of the creator of the universe right in their midst and did not even recognize it. They had the fulfillment of prophecy standing before them and were oblivious to the fact. The chances of one man's fulfilling even forty-eight Old Testament prophecies concerning the Messiah are one in 10^{157}.[1] The plan from the foundation of the world was about to be fulfilled right in front of their eyes. The salvation of mankind was about to be purchased for all eternity, and they were blind to it.

Jesus indicted them for not seeing the spiritual signs of the times. He called them hypocrites! God was about to do something spectacular, and they could not recognize it. We must begin to see the signs of the times in which we live. If we only look at what everyone else looks at, we could miss the impact of the incredible time in history in which we are living right now.

It is so easy to let the news media tell us what to make of the current state of our young people. We trust in the statistics of research specialists and allow them to chart our course instead of seeing the spiritual signs of the times and planning accordingly. Jesus called the people of His day hypocrites because they professed to be spiritually inclined, yet they planned their lives by physical signs.

When we go through life just following earthly signs, we may never realize we have a chance to make history. What a crime to be seized by destiny and not even know it!

The opportunity of a lifetime could be knocking at your door, but unless you see the signs of the times as God does you will not recognize the opportunity.

Today's Spiritual Signs

Could it be that we are in another season in history where God is about to do incredible things in the earth, and we cannot see it? Is it possible that the spiritual signs of the times are pointing to a great awakening in the twentieth century and we are oblivious to it?

We pride ourselves on our ability to see physical signs and make predictions. We can make a good guess at who is going to the NCAA final four and act like a seasoned prophet when we conclude from the six o'clock news, "This generation is going to the dogs." Are we so caught up by what seems obvious that we cannot see what God does?

Let's look at another set of statistics from a different point of view. The United Nations' most current estimate of the world's population is 5.572 billion people.[2] About 43 percent of these people are currently under twenty years of age.[3] Think about the ramifications for this generation of young people. Almost one-half of the world is the age of that wild rascal in your youth group — or younger.

We have a very young world. Most countries have an incredibly disproportionate number of young people and of babies being born.

Who is going to reach this young world? Is it the old people? In spite of the fact that there are many valuable ministries from older people for the children and youth of the world, God leaves each generation to evangelize itself. These ministries to the young will prepare and teach teens how to reach their own generation.

Almost half of the world is counting on your teenager. The eternal destiny of 2.4 billion people is in the hands of our youth groups!

Add to this the fact that more than 80 percent of the world's young people are raised in a non-Christian home,[4] and we have a potential catastrophe on our hands. We are in danger of an entire, new generation being untouched by the gospel. How will our young people respond in this critical time? How will we equip them for their call?

Let's not forget the Generation X phenomenon. This is a massive group of people who by very definition have no purpose — nothing to identify with, no cause to live for. How is it that a generation with such an incredible mandate on their lives has found no purpose? Has God diverted their sight from a hollow cause and preserved their energy for the cause He is about to show them?

We don't have to draw them away from another passion; they are an open generation, waiting for a cause.

This is our chance to give them something that demands their all — the only thing worth giving their all for. Their purpose can be found only in the call that God has placed on their lives. They have been sent providentially into the world "for such a time as this" (Esth. 4:14). You have providentially *happened* upon this book "for such a time as this." You are a leader or parent who has influence over young people "for such a time as this."

God knew the exact time that your young people were going to be born into this world. The season of openness to a war cry for a generation is right now! We have the opportunity to help them seize their moment in history. We can transform Generation X into a generation that takes the cross to the world.

The young people in our homes and churches have a unique *mandate on their lives*. This is not just a good idea or a casual suggestion. It is an *imperative*.

We may see them as pretty good kids who get into a little trouble now and then, but God sees them differently. All of heaven has been waiting for this moment in history. Christian young people have a unique opportunity. They can allow their non-Christian peers to dominate, or they can strike back with a revolution of radical Christianity.

It is time to embrace the challenge before them. There is no room for wallflower Christians who watch everyone else do the job. There is no plan B. Today's Christian young people are the only answer for this world's problems. God is counting on their obedience to answer that call. But He depends on us to prepare them for the challenge.

What Is Our Message?

When we call them to radical Christianity, what are we asking of them? Does giving it all to Jesus mean, "Come to church on Sundays and Wednesdays"? We ask them to do a variety of spiritual duties and activities, but why? What do we really want them to become? What does God want them to become?

The mandate for this generation means just one thing:

God calls today's young person to be a world-changer.

There is no room for compromise. There is no other option. God is counting on them to change this world.

World-changers will read their Bibles and spend time alone with God. World-changers stand strong against sin. They mature in Christ. We can use retreats, camps, choirs, fund-raisers, sleep-overs and a host of other *external* activities as preparation for our teens' *internal* activity — transformation to world-changer. God is counting on these young people.

We can help them grow by our own clear understanding of *what* we want from them and *why* we are asking them to do it. It is not enough to involve them in spiritual activities in the hope that something will stick with them.

It is time to quit hoping and start preparing them for war.

Using the Foolish to Confound the Wise

It would be easy to ask, "If this is true, then why have so many tragic things happened to teens today? How could God possibly use the brokenness of these emotionally crippled teens that the media has portrayed?"

Jesus' disciples saw a blind man and asked, "Rabbi, who sinned, this man or his parents, that he was born blind?" (John 9:2). Their question is echoed in the hearts of parents across the country who wonder, If God has such a great plan for my teen, then why the heartbreak? Why the hopelessness? Why all the tragedies?

Jesus' response set the stage for a miracle: " 'Neither this man nor his parents sinned,' said Jesus, 'but this happened so that the work of God might be displayed in his life' " (John 9:3). Jesus turned their focus from the tragedy to the miracle His Father was about to do. God wanted an opportunity to show His stuff — a chance to show the incredible greatness of His might and the magnitude of His love. God was about to display His healing character through something the devil had used to rob this man of wholeness.

He is about to do the same thing with this young generation. God wants to take the most unlikely people on the face of the earth and use them for His glory. No man will get the glory for His work — He will transform a purposeless generation into a world-changing movement. He wants to "bind up the brokenhearted" (Is. 61:1) and make a mighty army out of them. He will use the most underachieving, low SAT scorer to shape the eternal destiny of those with doctorate degrees. He will use the foolish things to confound the wise (1 Cor. 1:27).

NINE

GIVING THEM THE VISION

GOD WANTS TO accomplish some amazing things through this generation. We have been inundated by the media to accept the bleak evidence of the need for transformation. Look at the report of secular industry, which grabs the fifty-six billion dollars that teenagers spend annually.[1] The media tailor programs to grab teens' attention in order to get the advertising dollars. The typical fourteen-year-old watches three hours of TV but does only one hour of homework each day.[2] Teens are influenced more by TV than by schoolwork. This shapes their vision.

When asked what teens buy with their hard-earned dollars (or hard-begged from Mom and Dad), 81 percent of teens say they buy CDs and tapes.[3] These things shape the way they see life. MTV reaches twenty million people each week.[4] There are only twenty-four million teens in America, and MTV has almost all of them. No wonder it has become the advertising venue of choice for anyone who is trying to break into the teen market.

According to researchers who studied six hours of randomly taped MTV, about half of the videos on MTV contain sexually explicit references. Fifty percent have love and romance themes, 15 percent contain violence, and 13 percent depict conflict between parents and teenagers. The studies indicate that those who watched MTV were more likely to say that premarital sex and use of violence in videos is OK than those who hadn't seen MTV.[5] MTV has the power to influence fads, clothes, values and even votes.[6] Will we stand by and let MTV shape the vision and future of an entire generation?

A Prophetic Future

An overwhelming hope is sparked in our hearts as we watch destiny take its course. But wait a minute — did I say *watch?* Is that what we are called to do as adults?

For many years Christians have heard exhortations about how God is going to use the young people in the last days:

> And afterward, I will pour out my Spirit on all people. Your sons and daughters will prophesy, your old men will dream dreams, your young men will see visions (Joel 2:28).

Spiritual leaders have proclaimed, "The young people will be used to bring in the end-time revival." Youth camps and retreats across America sing out the anthem, "He is going to do a great thing — He will use the teens to touch the world."

It is easy to get caught up with what God is *going to do* with young people. But at the same time we have a great sense of urgency as we anticipate the incredible miracle that will bring this anthem to pass. We long to see it happen *now*. But we see no earthly reason to believe that today's young people will actually be the ones to facilitate a great revival.

It is easy to develop a spectator mentality, to sit back and *watch* what God is going to do. After all, if God said He would do it, then surely He is capable of bringing it to pass. So we sit in anticipation much as we wait for the start of a football game.

What Is My Role?

The fact that God wants to make world-changers of this generation makes us ask, "What is my responsibility?" Every adult believer must ask,

"How can I make a significant contribution to their preparation? How can I prepare them for what God wants to do?"

How does God want to use the older generation to help these teens stand up and fulfill their destiny? What is our role in parenting a world-changer? How is it different from parenting a pew-sitter? How can I be a *catalyst* for this end-time revival with teens? What part does God have for *me* to play?

Is God waiting for your involvement to initiate His strategy to affect the nations? Is this generation pausing before the battle because they need our input before they can begin fighting?

As parents and leaders we have the opportunity to plant a vision to change the world within the heart of a young person. We must be convinced of the mandate God has placed on his or her life. We must accept this as a personal calling as parents. God has put us in this world "for such a time as this" (Esth. 4:14). He has given us a family to raise and people to influence. He "determined the times set for them and the exact places where they should live" (Acts 17:26). He also set the design for how the world would be uniquely positioned to be reached by this young generation.

Jesus constantly poured His vision into His disciples. He tried to get them to see beyond themselves — to see the big picture. He wanted them to see the world the way God did and to find their place in His vision for it. Imagine Jesus — the only Son of the awesome living God — trying to get a bunch of ordinary humans to see what His Father sees on the landscape of humanity.

A Vision That Captures the Imagination

Jesus challenged His disciples to dare to imagine what God really wanted in their world. He challenges us to expand our concept of what He wants to happen in our world today.

He explained to His disciples that they were the "salt of the earth" and the "light of the world" (Matt. 5:13-14). His strategy was to make them agents of change in the world. Joining Jesus meant the disciples were on a quest to change the status quo.

In Matthew 8 Jesus marveled at the faith of the gentile centurion. He opened His disciples' minds to the fact that there would be many others who also would believe. He said, "Many will come from the east and the west, and will take their places at the feast with Abraham, Isaac, and Jacob in the kingdom of heaven" (v. 11). He was saying, "Open your eyes — this thing is big! It is bigger than Israel. It is as big as the world."

He taught them from parables such as the good shepherd who left the ninety-nine sheep to find one that was lost (Luke 15:4-7). "Got the picture yet? This is what My Father is like. He cares for the one no one else even knew was missing. He is relentless in His pursuit of the lost and hurting in this world."

In the parable about the wedding feast, the king issued many invitations for the rich and noble to come. But they would not. So He sent invitations for others to come, but they were not interested either.

Finally the king ordered his servant to go to the "roads and country lanes and make them come in" (Luke 14:23). This is the heart of the Father. He will do whatever it takes to get people to come into the kingdom. Jesus illustrated many different ways to plant the vision of the vastness of God's heart for the world into the thinking of His disciples.

He implored them to "ask the Lord of the harvest...to send out workers into His harvest field" (Matt. 9:38).

God's mandate to the youth of this generation is to bring a harvest of human souls into His kingdom. Jesus' followers were to be ready to impact the way others lived in this world. They were to be activists.

On another occasion He said, "What I tell you in the dark, speak in the daylight; what is whispered in your ear, proclaim from the housetops" (Matt. 10:27). The disciples were not guarding a well-kept secret — they were to proclaim to everyone the things He had told them.

Just like a football coach who sets his team's goals high, Jesus inspired His disciples with the idea of taking this message to the whole world. "And this gospel of the kingdom will be preached in the whole world as a testimony to all nations, and then the end will come" (Matt. 24:14). He commanded them to take it to the world as He issued the ultimate challenge of the Great Commission (see Matt. 28:19-20).

By following the example of Jesus we can find creative ways to get the message across to our young people. They must learn what the disciples learned. We can impact their perspective with the vision of the kind of followers they can be — we can teach them to think big.

In Jesus' day, and in the life of the early church, normal Christianity called for everyone to be involved in reaching the world with the gospel. Being a world-changer was not an option; it was just part of the package. That kind of Christianity should be the norm for today's youth also — and for us, the older generation.

A Vision That Demands Their All

When Jesus communicated the vastness of the job, He also communicated the degree of commitment it would take. The job He was calling them to was so big it would require their all. It was so important it was worthy of their all.

Just as a football coach demands a total commitment to the endless running of wind sprints, Jesus also has high demands. The coach does not apologize for the exacting demands he places on his team because he knows his goals require it. Even though his players may not like the exercise routines at first, every player who has ever won a championship game returns to thank the coach for being so tough on him.

Jesus wants everyone to come to Him on His terms. When someone said to Jesus, "Lord, first let me go and bury my father," Jesus told him, "Let the dead bury their own dead, but you go and proclaim the kingdom of God" (Luke 9:59-60). Jesus' response was basically, "Save it, Bud. If you are coming to Me on your terms, don't come."

Another time He said, "On my account you will be brought before governors and kings as witnesses to them and to the Gentiles. But when they arrest you, do not worry about what to say or how to say it. At that time you will be given what to say" (Matt. 10:18-19). His imperative was: Go ahead and plan on doing whatever it takes to get the job done. No matter what you have to go through, the cost is worth it. He was building the fiber of character in them that could withstand anything.

Remember how He said, "No one who puts his hand to the plow and looks back is fit for service in the kingdom of God" (Luke 9:62)? Another said to Him, "I will follow you wherever you go." Jesus replied, "Foxes have holes and birds of the air have nests, but the Son of Man has no place to lay his head" (Luke 9:57-58).

Do you really want to follow Him? Then be ready to do anything.

Jesus likened the kingdom of heaven to a treasure hidden in a field and a pearl of great value. When a man found these he "sold everything" to get them (Matt. 13:44-46). The value of what He offered was worth everything they owned. It still is.

This vision will separate peripheral Christians from those who want to make a difference in the world. If we make serving the Lord look "easy," we water down what He demanded of His own disciples. Do we dare ask less of Jesus' followers than He did Himself? He is the One to set the standard of what He desires.

It may surprise us to discover that our young people are more ready to give their all than we had thought. They are just waiting to find a vehicle of ministry (such as missions or evangelism) to pour themselves into. Let us be like the coach who unashamedly asks so much of his team that he knows they may decide to leave.

*Let's give this generation the dignity
to decide for themselves whether
or not they will rise to the occasion
and fulfill their mandate.*

A Vision for Our Family

To communicate this world-changing mentality to our young people, we must be convinced that God wants to use our family to change the world. With determination, our families can make their mark on this world. Our anthem is: "My family will do something that counts for eternity." We cannot afford one wasted life or one wasted family.

When our kids are young we can teach them how people around the world need to know Jesus. Books like Patrick Johnstone's *Operation World* and Jill Johnstone's *You Can Change the World*[7] are excellent tools to get your children involved in praying for the world and interested in reaching it from their earliest years.

Planting this vision doesn't begin only when they are teens. Each night my wife, Katie, and I read something about the children of the world to our three- and four-year-old girls. I have felt goosebumps more than once as my four-year-old prays with authority: "And, devil, we bind you from these children. You can't have them. Jesus, send someone to reach them and tell them You love them."

A compassionate, caring lifestyle
will communicate to our children
that we are living for more
than ourselves.

We will not be consumed by secular attractions but will live with passion to make a difference for Christ in this world.

God's army is broken into squadrons and companies just as our military forces are divided. We can catch a glimpse of these units through the many different denominations and churches reaching different groups of people. The smallest unit of the church is the family. Dad is the commander-in-chief, and Mom is the chief-of-staff.

The whole unit goes to war every day. Little Johnny goes off to school to witness to the bully, while Jeannie is commissioned to junior high for the day to reach out to her friend whose family is going through a divorce. These young ones are in training to take on the world! Every day they fight the battle for people's souls and prepare to take over the world.

Mom is involved in reaching people within her sphere of influence, while Dad may witness to his boss. At the end of the day we gather to hear the war stories of what God did through each member.

This is the family at work in the kingdom of God. These are God's platoons, building the resilience of a world-changer.

What will our family stand for? What do we want to be known for? What legacy will you leave as a family? Will you stand for more than family reunions and family picnics? Will you be known for more than a swing set and a family dog? Will anyone remember you for more than being the good people down the street? When you are old, will family photo albums and home videos be your legacy, or will your family be remembered as one that made its mark on the world while it had the chance? Right now is the time to seize the moment.

Let us fill our kids' hearts with the same kind of vision that Jesus gave His disciples. Let us challenge them with a vision that demands their all and entreats them to rise to the occasion and fulfill their call. Let us be the ones who take seriously the conviction that our families must make a significant difference for Christ in this world.

TEN

BELIEVING IN THEIR POTENTIAL

THANK YOU FOR believing in us!" These words are inscribed in countless letters I receive from teenagers all across America. These young people are starved for someone to respect the ability they possess to change the world. As we have taken thousands of them overseas, they have gained a glimpse of the potential God has instilled in them. These trips helped them to see themselves beyond the mistrust and lack of confidence that come from an older generation that finds it difficult to imagine what the world will be like when these young ones are running it.

Potential in Your Kids

Parenting is largely undefined for many parents. Just what is the real goal of rearing a child? Especially as a Christian? Of course we will feed and clothe them, teach them responsibility and hope they make something out of their lives. But what is that "something" we are hoping for? How can we help them find the *thing* that God wants for them?

We must ask ourselves, What do I really want for my kids? Perhaps you answer, "I want them to be on fire for God," or "I want them to be radical for Jesus." What does that mean? Some parents believe their job is done if their teen makes it out of high school without abusing drugs or becoming pregnant. Others think they have done a pretty good job if their son or daughter moves off to college without too much rebellion or too many problems.

Some parents and leaders even look forward to the day when Johnny won't be in the youth group anymore to "cause problems."

What is the goal of my leadership? my parenting? What do I want for the future of the teens I influence? Will I be satisfied if they go to college, join a Christian campus club and still go to church? Is my ultimate dream for them to find a good job in corporate America and be a good Christian witness?

God is raising up a generation that does not blend

in with the rest of the world. Can you visualize your college-age youth sharing his faith to the point that revival breaks out? Can you imagine so many members of secular campus clubs (such as gay and lesbian clubs) being saved through his influence that the club leaders persecute and ridicule him? What if his homework papers made so many references to God that his atheistic professors threatened to kick him out of their classes?

Your college graduate son or daughter could be the one who starts a morning devotional time to disciple his fellow workers at his new job. What would happen if all his co-workers fell on their knees in repentance after he shared his faith with them?

Can you imagine your teenager refusing to compromise his integrity at his fast-food restaurant job and going to his boss to stand up for his faith? Imagine his getting fired because of it. What a legacy to have! Or imagine his boss getting saved and giving him a raise!

We have to see the potential of the lives we influence. Everyone must be trained as a world-changer. This does not mean that everyone has to be a missionary (although at least one overseas missionary trip sometime is a great idea), but everyone must make an impact on the world.

Our young people's mission should be to infiltrate their secular workplaces with the gospel of Jesus Christ. This is their real work.

Imagine parents and youth pastors preparing their young people as agents to infiltrate enemy camps. We must raise a generation that launches into their adult lives with a different agenda.

As this objective becomes clear, we will concentrate our energies on things that transform these kids into awesome, incredible world-changers.

Your first impulse may be to doubt that your child, or your youth group, can change the world. *Learn to see their potential as God does.*

You may see your teen writing notes in youth group or making spit wads in church. He may fight with his brothers and sisters when they are home. You may wonder how your teen could change the world when you can't even get him to change his sheets. God sees all that stuff too, yet He still believes in his potential — and He is still counting on him.

When you add to what you see all the things the world says about this generation, it is not hard to be discouraged. We hear about the "dumbing of America." A popular commentator on Christian radio says they have "mush for brains." When descriptions like the following appear, it is easy to give up hope:

> ...a group that is said to be politically disengaged and politically correct, obsessed with surfaces and addicted to irony, scarred by Watergate and Vietnam and unaware of them, technologically savvy and unconditionally ignorant, busy saving the planet and craving electricity and noise, prematurely careerist and proud to be lazy, unwilling to grow up and too grown up already.[1]

In spite of this, MTV still believes in them. At least

they believe enough in their revenue potential to build an entire network around their culture. Could it be that MTV believes in the potential of our young people more than we as Christian parents do?

We have got to decide whether we will believe what the world says or what the Word of God says about our kids.

Seeing Below the Surface

The Bible tells how Jesus came to the shores of Galilee one day and ministered to the people. He asked Peter if He could use his boat to preach from. Fishermen were not at the top of the social hierarchy of that day, to say the least. They were poor and worked very hard for a living. Peter's boat was not a yacht. It was probably beat up, with chipped or no paint and covered with repaired spots on its sides. Even though it was neither new nor beautiful, the Son of God wanted to use it.

God wants to use our kids no matter what they have been through — just like Peter's boat. He will use whatever we have to offer Him. Even if the struggles of life have messed up our young people, God still wants to restore them and use them.

Peter gladly let Jesus use his boat, and afterward Jesus asked Peter to go out into the deeper waters to fish. At first Peter did not want to go, but he obeyed Jesus' request. As a result Peter filled not only his own boat but his friend's boat as well with an incredible catch of fish. As they were coming back to shore it dawned on Peter that this was no ordinary day of fishing. He realized that a miracle had taken place right before his eyes.

Luke describes what happened when Peter returned to Jesus:

> When Simon Peter saw this, he fell at Jesus' knees and said, "Go away from me, Lord; I am a sinful man!" For he and all his companions were astonished at the catch of fish they had taken (Luke 5:8).

A simple response from Jesus changed Peter's life forever. His destiny seized him as he heard these words from Jesus' lips.

> Then Jesus said to Simon, "Don't be afraid; from now on you will catch men." So they pulled their boats up on shore, left everything and followed Him (Luke 5:10-11).

Can you picture Peter's appearance? He was probably a hairy guy, ruddy and dirty, and had not used his Safeguard soap for a while. He may have had a tooth or two missing, and his clothes were most likely soiled and torn. There were not a lot of physical reasons to believe he would ever make much of his life. Yet Jesus saw below the surface — He saw something inside Peter that would make him great in the kingdom of God.

When Peter dumped all those fish up on shore, he was astounded at Jesus' miracle. Perhaps that is when the words Jesus spoke began to sink into his spirit:

"Fish? You want fish? Let me tell you something, Peter. You were not made to fish for fish. You were made to fish for men. One day you will catch more men than all the fish you ever caught. I see something great in you, Peter. One day you will preach to a crowd of three thousand, and their lives will be changed. You will bring healing to a lame man at the gate Beautiful. You will help start churches where people have never heard the good news of God's love. You will even write God's words for millions of believers to read in the future. I see a lot of potential in you, Peter!"

Jesus could see in Peter what Peter could not see in himself.

Jesus saw purpose, vision and destiny. Can you see that in your teens?

Can you see the seed of greatness that God put in your youth group? Can you look past the rough edges of their habits and attitudes to see what Jesus sees in them?

It is easy to identify the areas where our kids are doing poorly. It is easy to predict the failure of this generation by listening to society's descriptions. It seems natural to degrade our teens as they constantly fall below our expectations. Many teens are reminded of their probable failure by their own parents.

Parents have prophesied over their kids with negative words: "You will probably be flipping burgers your whole life." "You'll never amount to a hill of beans." "You can't do anything right." These same parents act so surprised when their negative predictions prove true. "I told you you would end up at a burger stand for a career," the parents recount, glorying in their accuracy at predicting the future.

A poll was taken of men in prison, asking, "How many of you were told by your parents that you would end up in prison one day?" Ninety-eight percent of the men polled said their parents had told them that was what would happen.

We need to affirm the positive potential that God has given to our youth — we need to see them as God sees them.

I have heard the cries of teens who are looking for their parents' acceptance and approval. We asked teens to tell us which of their parents' statements have stuck in their minds. Read their responses:

- You're a nothing and will never amount to anything.

- You'll never make it in life because you are stupid.

- I wouldn't be surprised if you end up drunk on the street someday.

- I hate you; you aren't worth anything.

- You're fat.

- You're a problem.

- You're a mistake.

- You are a loser and will fail at anything you do.

- I wish you had never been born.

- You get on my nerves.

- If we didn't have you kids we would be rich.

- I don't love you.

- You will never be anything but average.

- Go to hell.

- All you're going to do is mess up.

- I wish you weren't my son.

- It is your fault that we divorced.

- You were not planned. We wanted a boy, and if we had had the money you would have been aborted.

- You have ruined my life.

- You were a mistake, and we never really wanted you in the first place.

- I wish you were dead.

Can you hear the heart of a generation of teens who feel that even their own parents do not believe in them?

Jesus knew exactly what He wanted Peter to become — a fisher of men. He was not hoping aimlessly that people would follow Him and get closer to God. He set out to *make* world-changers. We do not have to plan our kid's future and force him into a specific career. We do need to teach him the principles of the kind of person God is calling him to be. He must be a world-changer. Jesus made no bones about it, and neither should we.

Jesus' words shocked Peter. In response, Peter dropped everything to follow Him. Jesus actually *believed* in him. When our young people find someone who believes in them, they will do anything for that person. That's the reason pimps are able to get attractive young girls to work the streets and do whatever they ask.

Our young people need to know we have discovered the seeds of greatness within them. When they finally find someone who recognizes their potential, they will abandon the direction this world has given them. When they see an older generation that is *convinced* of their potential, there is nothing they won't do to fulfill that potential.

ELEVEN

FINDING IDENTITY AND BELONGING IN THE CALL

HOW WOULD TODAY'S teens respond to the questions "What are you into?" or "What do you do?" Would they respond, "Music," "sports," "hanging out" or "skating"? These would be some of the most common answers. How many would answer, "God," "church" or "the Bible"? If you guessed not many, you are right.

When we asked teens across North America, "What is your purpose?" we received these responses:

- I am not sure.

- To protect America.

- To become a pro sports person.

- To make the world into something fun.

- To add to the statistics.

Some young people are starting to take life a little more seriously by finding something meaningful to pour their lives into. As one teen in Ohio put it, "I used to say, 'Just let me lead my own life.' But now I look around and see a world that needs me."[1] This youth was speaking from a secular point of view. The problems of the world are being noticed by teens, and they are seeking to be part of the solution. Some are predicting that saving the environment will be a uniting force or that teaching will be the peace corps of the nineties.[2] The point remains that they are looking for something to stand up for.

Even though these same kids may have attended church all their lives, they do not identify church as *what they are into*. They might go, but it is just a peripheral activity to their lives — maybe even a forced activity. It is not what gives them passion and purpose.

Check the Perception

The youth group is perceived by many, even by adults, as a peripheral activity — a necessary evil in

---

some cases. It represents "just another activity" to many parents who have to run their kids all over town for other secular activities. The youth group is sort of a by-product of the "big church" and must be maintained in order to keep everyone happy. It is another addition to the already busy church calendar of events and services. The main Sunday service is for adults, and all the other ministries have been designed to keep the constituents happy. Usually the youth department is one of those ministries.

If this is the kind of perception that parents and church leaders have regarding the youth department, how can we expect the teens to value it more?

I look forward to the day when thousands of teens will thunder in reply to the question "What are you into?" with the response: "I am into God. I serve Him with all my heart. He is the only way to real life. He set me free, turned me on and gave me a new life. You need to get into God too; He will change you too!"

The problem goes below the surface. The teens respond based on what is most important to them. Though they go to church and youth group, what they are really into may be something quite different.

What they are into is the thing that takes up all their time and where they find most of their friends. Their identity and definition come from this source, it tells them who they are.

Everyone Needs Belonging

Everyone needs a place to belong — a place where they fit in. Young people especially, trying to discover who they are, are looking for a group to interact with that will help them define themselves. Adolescents long inwardly for relationships that give a sense of security.

This desperate drive for inclusion among teens is what compels them to participate in many different wild activities. When the sense of belonging is missing, particularly in the home, young people will find other places to belong. Hence the growth of street gangs in America with all their initiation procedures and rites of passage to gain entrance. *World Book Encyclopedia* defines street gangs as "adolescent organizations that are usually based on ethnic solidarity and neighborhood allegiance." According to *World Book*, when young people join a gang they are looking for

> respect, loyalty and solidarity; intimacy and a 'family' feeling; status and power; security and protection; social life; economic advantage and maintenance of ethnic tradition or culture." In 1965, police departments in only fifteen of the nation's one hundred largest cities had reported the presence of street gangs. By 1992, that number had grown to at least ninety-two of those cities, the greatest proliferation occurring in the latter half of the 1980s. The U.S. Department of Justice estimated that in 1991 there were 4,881 gangs nationwide, with 249,324 members.[3]

Other Activities That Bring Belonging

Most of the time young people feel the place they fit in best is among fellow team members in a sport, a band or a club at school. Some end up fitting in only with all the other misfits. These young people usually become rebellious, distancing themselves from others by their hair, clothes, music and drugs.

How can it be that these kids have been in church since they were born yet find their sense of belonging outside the church walls and away from their church friends?

This is why so many have "school friends" and "church friends," and never the twain shall meet. Their identity is wrapped up in something totally separate from the purpose of God for their lives. What an incredible tragedy to be reared around the things of God for their entire lifetime, yet have their hearts captured by a seemingly innocent secular activity.

Belonging to the Cause

You can identify a young person's priority when a conflict arises in activity schedules. The one that inevitably gets chosen is the place of security. The one that is always "accidentally" forgotten is lower on the totem pole. When you ask a teen what he is into, who he is comes out. You get a glimpse of what he is really made of and which group of people it is important for him to be around.

God's desire is that we all find our belonging and identity in His kingdom and in what He wants us to do. He does not want to be just another activity in our lives — He wants to be our very life. Everything we are should be wrapped up in Him and the purpose for which He has put us in this world.

More church or youth activities are not the answer. This attitude misses the core of the issue. Because many parents get more gratification from watching their kids perform on the football field or in the school drama, they are more motivated to continue taking them to school activities than to church functions.

Thus the young people pick up on what pleases their parents and are more likely to choose these activities. The parents also find belonging among the other parents of kids in that activity.

Take sports, for example. Dad may have a lot more fun and find more camaraderie with the other fathers of the team members than with the other fathers of the kids at the youth group. Thus he reinforces his son's craving for those activities. Think about it. When was the last time you complimented your teenage son or daughter on memorizing a scripture or dealing with an area of character in his or her life?

We should model and lead them to the kind of Christianity that will make them *want* to identify with the Christian lifestyle. The sports coach does not have to beg the kids to join. There is already a perception that draws the young person into his camp.

Our youth need a Christian faith which is worth their identifying with.

If being a Christian is merely an addendum to *your* life, your teens will never allow *their* lives to revolve around it. As we present a vision that demands their all, their commitment to it will begin to consume their entire lives.

Moses' Youth Group

Moses had a youth group of about three million people. They were not unlike most teens in the church today. These young Jews had heard of the God of Abraham, Isaac and Jacob, but they did not know much about Him. They had heard of Noah and the rainbow, but they did not know Noah's God. They had been in slavery for four hundred years. They were a scattered and diverse people. Moses' job was to pull them together and help them discover who they were and where they were going.

Though most young people today have heard of the Lord, they do not know their potential in Him. They have become so familiar with the talk about Him that it is no longer meaningful to them. They have lost the purpose for their relationship with Him. In fact, even the words "personal relationship with Christ" carry little or no meaning. Their Christian life consists of a summation of overused, meaningless rhetoric that somehow, when used in the right way, is supposed to keep them close to God and out of hell.

Moses had no small chore on his hands. He had to define for the children of Israel who they were and what they were supposed to be about. The Ten Commandments were a part of that process. More than just a bunch of rules, they defined the Israelites' priorities as a people.

The first four related to the kind of relationship they

were to have with God. They were to have no other gods before Him and were to keep the Sabbath day holy (see Ex. 20:3,8). This is the kind of priority God wanted to have in their lives.

The other commandments defined who they were: a people who did not lie, steal or commit adultery as the rest of the world did; a people who did not kill each other as others did. God was imparting His divine values in His chosen people. He was helping to define them — to distinguish them as a people separate from the rest of the world.

All the levitical and ceremonial rules can be seen as further clarification of the Israelites as a people. "Honor your father and your mother" invoked respect and honor for the elders of the community. If disobeyed, it carried a penalty of death by stoning (see Deut. 21:18-21). They were to be a responsible people. They were required to make restitution when a neighbor's animal was injured on someone else's property (see Ex. 22:14). They were not to be a perverted nation like the rest of the world, for God commanded, "Do not have sexual relations with an animal" (Lev. 18:23).

These Israelites were commanded to celebrate three different feasts a year, each one a week long (see Lev. 23). They were to be a people who knew how to party! God wanted them to be a people who knew how to cut loose and have a great time!

It was Moses' responsibility to teach these rules to the Israelites and to write them down. Their survival as a nation depended on their ability to grasp who God wanted them to be.

The Blessing of Isolation

Being out in the wilderness for such a long time was more of a blessing than they thought.

They were away from the rest of the world long enough to learn of their own distinctiveness.

Shaping the Identity of Our Kids

As parents and leaders we need to provide the same kind of clarity for our young people today as they wander back and forth to church, school and home. By understanding the mandate on their lives, they will be drawn into belonging to the call on their generation.

All that we say and do must echo this mandate. They are God's army — called to win the world for Him. They must follow the principles by which they are called to live.

Time + Intensity = Identity

Most of the time a coach or band instructor defines these things more clearly than the church does. This is why our young people often find more belonging in sports or other activities. A coach demands commitment and time. As a result, the teen's identity is wrapped up in that activity. Many times we are afraid of asking more of our kids, thinking it will scare them away. We fear they will not want to come to youth group or church anymore. All the while, we are not realizing that commitment is one of the very things that draws them into finding their belonging in a group.

A teen finds identity through the music he listens to constantly. His sense of belonging is wrapped up in the friends he hangs around with. Time spent equals identification. Granted, time is not the only key. It would be a fallacy to think that forcing your teen to church and youth group every time the doors are open would make him want to be there more. There must be something there for him to identify with, something in which to sink his teeth.

Just as the forty years in the wilderness helped to define the purpose of the Israelites, we can utilize times of isolation to help our teens understand their purpose in life. That is one reason why camps, retreats and mission trips are so useful for teenagers. It gives them a chance to get away from the world and get used to their distinctiveness.

They develop relationships with others who share the same identity, and as they get closer to the Lord He reinforces who they are supposed to be.

We can, and should, take our teens to church.

If we are going to capture their belonging and identity, we must capture their hearts and minds.

We can only capture their hearts and minds if we give them something worth their commitment. The gospel is more than just another obligation in life — it is worth our total commitment.

PART FOUR

WHAT GOD IS DOING
WITH TEENAGERS TODAY

So why all the despair about today's
young people? Oh, I know we never hear on the
CBS news what God is doing through young
people. Even on Christian TV it is rare to get
a complete, accurate picture of what is
happening with today's teens.
Despite the gloomy picture painted
by the world, a number of significant events
indicate a movement of teens into the kingdom.
Get ready to move over as these radicals
come blasting through with a rage of modern
revival in the style of a nineties teenager.

TWELVE

THE SPIRITUAL AWAKENING OF TEENS IN THE NINETIES

GOD IS SHAKING the foundations of our youth. Everywhere I go I hear teens expressing their dissatisfaction with the "hype Christianity" that has been so prevalent among teenagers. The spiritual roller coaster experience is getting old. They are sick of "warm fuzzies" and goose bumps — then going on with life as if there were no God. They can spot fake

Christianity a mile away. Because it is so prevalent, they have been tempted to go along with it. But as many of us adults have found, the fake hype only endures for a short season. It forces a choice: Will it become a part of your lifestyle, will you just quit trying to be a Christian, or will you accept the challenge to discover the *real* thing?

Young people are tired of seeing the hypocritical imitation of Christianity from adults and peers. Disdain for this halfhearted brand of Christianity is emerging.

They Believe

According to Gallup, 95 percent of American teens believe in God, and 93 percent believe that God loves them. About 76 percent believe in angels, and 86 percent believe that Jesus is God, or the Son of God. This is a great step in the right direction. God is beginning to capture the hearts and minds of these young people. Gallup also says that 36 percent of all teens in America read their Bible at least once a week, and 40 percent believe religion is increasing in influence in American life.

In addition, 42 percent of teens say they pray alone frequently, and more than one-third (36 percent) of the teenagers in the United States belong to a church youth group. Up to 45 percent say they attended a church or synagogue in the last week. Hope is not lost — far from it. There are many who are still in one way or another under the influence of a church environment.[1]

A Radical Prayer Force

The most excitement comes from what is happening outside the context of the traditional youth group.

You may have heard about the "See You at the Pole" event in the last few years. This is an annual event sponsored by a number of youth organizations and denominations to rally teens to gather at the flagpole before school starts on a set day in September. For the last two years more than a million teens have gathered around their flagpoles to pray for their schools. This means that over 5 percent of teens in America are praying overtly for revival in their schools.[2] The Barna Research Group found that 1,025,770 students participated in the 1993 See You at the Pole.[3]

See You at the Party

In March 1993 a number of denominations and youth organizations linked up to what they titled "Operation Power Link: See You at the Party." About a million teenagers invited more than 500,000 friends to pizza parties in homes around the country. During the event they watched a live broadcast on Trinity Broadcasting Network hosted by Josh McDowell. They reported that 80,000 young people came to Christ that night![4]

Moral Purity

The Southern Baptist Convention has been responsible for starting a campaign called "True Love Waits"

111

that has spread to a number of different denominations and parachurch organizations. This is a movement to get teens to wait until marriage for sexual intimacy. They also encourage a "second virginity" for those who have already blown it, urging them to stay pure until their wedding night. Tens of thousands of teens have signed commitment cards already, and the SBC is expecting up to 500,000 teens to commit to absolute purity by the summer of 1994![5]

Missions Mania

In the midst of selfish teenage America, we are seeing teens give their lives away to reach others. They are giving up the comforts of their usual lifestyles to share the gospel with people around the world. Instead of lying out by the pool and getting tan, they are hiking up mountains in remote areas of the world so they can lie on the floor of a hut in a village full of people who have never known Christ. Instead of working to earn money to spend on foolish things, they are raising money so they can go overseas to work for the kingdom of God — spreading the gospel and harvesting souls.

Over the past seven years, Teen Mania's outreach teams have grown by 60 percent each year. More and more teens are signing up to give their lives away. We have helped thousands of normal, red-blooded adolescents to do something radical in nations around the world. They have started churches, ministered in prisons and brought the gospel to remote tribes — many of whom never had a chance to hear the gospel before the teens came. They have literally made history! We have documented over 300,000 people who have come to know the Lord through *teens* over these past few years.

In addition, a lot of other groups are catching the missions fever for teens. I have seen dozens of missions organizations for teens sprout up in the past few years. Several denominations (including Baptists and Methodists) have contacted us about helping them to start their own teen missions programs. Dozens of churches call us on a regular basis wanting to know how to start a youth missions program for their group or wanting us to train their youth in drama so they can take it overseas. Many other teen mission groups are offering opportunities for ministry to our teens:

- *Youth for Christ* offers two- to three-week opportunities through evangelism, construction, music and drama.

- *Youth With a Mission* has been operating since 1964 and offers a variety of programs for short-term service year-round.

- *YUGO Ministries* provides week-long evangelistic outreach opportunities for youth to minister in the country of Mexico.

- *Royal Servants International* is an intense discipleship program where students share the gospel through music, puppets, drama, clowning and mime.

- *Calvary Commission* has been involved in prison ministry, urban ministry, foreign missions and strategic missions training since 1977.

- *Life Changers* focuses on church planting, evangelism and discipleship.

- *Delta Ministries International* offers summer trips for two to eleven weeks in Austria, France, Japan, Spain, Italy and Argentina.

Bible Club Phenomena

The Supreme Court ruling to take prayer out of the public schools may have backfired. This is similar to the situation in communist China where they expelled all the missionaries and outlawed Christianity in the 1950s. There were approximately five million Christians in 1949, and now with all the persecution there are an estimated seventy-five million Christians in China! In the same way, prohibition of prayer in U.S. schools is provoking a move toward God. Just tell a teen not to do something, and you can almost guarantee he will try. The interesting point to this whole phenomenon is that it is spearheaded by teens, not adults.

Another recent event is also spurring an uprising among these up-and-coming radicals. In 1988 a young woman named Bridget Mergens wanted to have a Bible club in her high school. She was sixteen years old and thought that if other students were allowed to have clubs in their areas of interest, she should be allowed to also. But her principal and superintendent disagreed. She pushed the issue until Christian author and attorney Jay Sekulow got involved to defend her. Then the case attracted national attention. It went all the way to the Supreme Court, which ruled in her favor. The equal access ruling states:

"It shall be unlawful for any public secondary school which receives Federal financial assistance and which has a limited open forum to deny equal access or a fair opportunity to, or discriminate against, any students who wish to conduct a meeting within that limited open forum on the basis of religious, political, philosophical, or other content of the speech at such meetings. (A public secondary school has a limited open forum whenever such a school grants an offering to or opportunity for one or more noncurriculum related student groups to meet on school premises during noninstructional time.)[6]

Bridget had graduated from high school by the time the court ruled, but it was not too late for thousands of other high school teens to claim a victory from the ruling. The word got out that it was legal to have your own Bible club on campus as long as it was *student-led and student-organized.* Booklets were published and distributed for the purpose of letting teens know their rights. (Please see the Appendix for more information about students' rights, starting Bible clubs and other student-led activities on campuses in the United States.)

Soon others who had followed the case latched onto the victory and proceeded to start their own Bible clubs. Quite a few of these clubs met with opposition because many school administrators were still in the dark about the Supreme Court ruling. Jay Sekulow and his army of lawyers at the American Center for Law and Justice stepped in to help and offered to defend any teen in America who has been denied the right to have a Bible club.

Teens began to see that they had the power to do something revolutionary for God. Hundreds took the risk and started clubs on their campuses. The latest estimates suggest that there are approximately nine thousand Bible clubs currently active on high school campuses in America. All of these are student-led.

Something is beginning to stir in America's youth.

Think of it: Up to nine thousand teenage activists have enough righteous indignation to push the issue in their local schools until they can start their own Bible clubs.

Passion to Reach Their Schools

Many of these teens have a genuine passion to reach their schools for Christ. They position themselves strategically to invade their schools with the message of the gospel. For example, two teenage guys came back from a Teen Mania missions trip with some creative ideas for ministering to their peers. They had business cards printed with their names and the phone number of a pager which they carried at all times. Wherever they went, they passed out their cards, telling people to call any time they needed help or prayer. They receive calls on a regular basis, praying for friends and leading them to Christ.

There is also the story of George, a pastor's son from the Houston area who had fallen away from the

Lord and joined a gang. As a last resort, the father sent his son to Argentina to live for a while with some relatives who were also involved in the ministry. When the boy arrived, he sensed the presence of God so intensely that all he could do was weep for a week. He became radically committed to Christ and asked a friend in the gang to come to Argentina for a visit. His friend had the same experience. They both returned home and proceeded to win their fellow gang members to the Lord.

A high school in a neighboring district was nicknamed Suicide High because five or six students at that school had killed themselves in the past year. George and several of his ex-gang member friends began to pray for the other school. George had a radical idea — they would transfer to the other school. After convincing their parents of their mission, several transferred schools. They believed God wanted them to be missionaries to their peers at the rival school.[7]

God is inspiring young people to do things that do not appear logical or rational. The key is that the decision to change schools was student-initiated. There is something about getting the idea yourself that brings ownership to an opportunity. We as adults cannot assume that we can think up all the ideas needed to facilitate the fire among these radical teens whom God is raising up.

We need to move over and let God give the young people of today their own dreams and visions about how to reach their world.

This missionary passion among high school students to reach their peers is in stark contrast to what is happening at the college level. Although there are a number of Christian colleges and Christian groups on secular campuses, there does not appear to be the same passion among the students to reach their peers.

College students have access to a number of Christian programs and opportunities, but most activities are controlled and planned by adults. The students themselves do not seem to have a deep yearning for God or a desire to do something radical for the sake of Christ.

Isn't it just like God to use the foolish things to confound the wise (1 Cor. 1:27)? He is gaining possession of the hearts of teens before education turns them toward a cerebral assent to the gospel message. Cerebral assent allows intellectual agreement with what the Bible says but not a personal experience with Christ. God is bypassing the cognitive kind of Christianity that acts as if there is a personal relationship with Christ yet never experiences His intimacy. He is drawing youth to embrace the cause of Christ with their hearts, and then He sends them to get their education to help further the cause.

Arenas Packed With Teens Seeking God

I have seen tens of thousands of young people crying out to God at our Acquire the Fire youth conventions all over North America. It is amazing to see teens respond to bold, relatable teaching of the Word and the evidenced presence of God.

Here are some of the things that teens in grassroots America are saying about Acquire the Fire and about their relationship with God:

- "I was amazed to see so many young people on fire for God! I got rid of unforgiveness and got relationships worked out, and, most of all, I got closer to God."
  — Rachel Whitby

- "Acquire the Fire was a spiritual awakening for me."
  — Heather Threatt

- "This was the second year I attended ATF. Not only did I forgive, but I learned to love in the craziest of situations."
  — Cody Murphy

- "The presence of God was like nothing I had ever felt before."
  — Tony D'Anza

- "An eye-opening and life-changing realization!"
  — Jamey Dixon

- "I have never seen so many teenagers on fire, sold out, radical and totally committed to the Lord.... I have a relationship with God, and He isn't just an acquaintance."
  — Mandy Morris

During the conventions we give the teens a chance to win a free music tape if they memorize enough

Scripture. They must quote the verses to our interns or staff to receive the tape. Some have been reported as coming up to quote the verses again and again to prove they are not just doing it to get the tape, but that they are getting it in their hearts.

One girl attended the New Orleans convention only because her mother made her come. When the convention ended, she told us that God had changed her life that weekend.

A youth leader from Dallas reported, "One girl came from my youth group who was in total rebellion against her parents and church. She was drinking, smoking and running around. She came not expecting anything. During the weekend she went forward to get her relationship with her parents and with God made right. She was totally changed, and you could see a definite change in her face."

At a conference in Ontario, Canada, a girl came to the altar with this prayer, "God, if You don't show me who You are and make Yourself real to me, I will serve the devil." God met this girl, changed her and showed her His awesome power. She is now serving God with all her heart!

I have challenged young people to commit to a consistent quiet time with God every day. Many of them have risen to the occasion and also committed to read through the Bible in one year.

Stephanie Roberts wrote after attending an ATF: "I think it's important for all teens (and adults) to spend some quiet time with the Lord. He can speak to you so you can get an understanding of His plan for your life."

Another young man wrote to say he had given up secular rap music. He thanked Teen Mania for teaching him how to say no to unholy things.

Still another wrote,

"God is doing so much for me.
I am seeking Him like never before.
This year I am going to focus totally
on God. I'm going to date God!"

Even parents are writing to tell us what is happening with their kids. One father said that his daughter was typically up and down in her relationship with Christ, but "she experienced something that weekend that changed her life. She now has a boldness and determination to serve the Lord no matter what."

Youth pastors tell us about the fiery passion that has ignited their youth groups after the convention. The spiritual fire in their own hearts has been rekindled as they witness even the hardest of hearts experience a dramatic rebirth. One youth pastor told of bringing a group of forty unsaved visitors along to a conference with his group of teens. He reported that thirty-seven of those visitors were saved during the weekend!

As you can see, there are many reasons to have optimism that God is about to do something great. There is a stirring among today's teens. Could it be a holy precursor of what is about to come? I do not know, but I have a hunch we are on to something big.

THIRTEEN

Real-Life World-Changers

Every time I stand in front of a group of teenagers, I look at each face. Some of them seem to be ready to burst with excitement for the Lord. Others act bored, annoyed or "too cool" to pay attention to what I'm saying. But I've learned one thing: I can't touch their hearts the way the Lord can. I have seen hundreds of young people encounter God for themselves and change in ways that neither I nor their parents ever dreamed of. Here are just a few examples.

Diana Disbrow and Jeremy Isom

Diana was a thirteen-year-old cheerleader with a bratty attitude, and she carried a mighty feisty stick. Jeremy was the fourteen-year-old son of a preacher, very church-wise. These two had gone to the meetings all weekend where we'd ministered in Maryland and had seemed to enjoy it, though they also had their own agenda for being there — to hang around with their friends.

Diana and Jeremy both said they wanted to take an overseas missions trip with us that summer. Had we known that Jeremy was the dread of every Sunday school teacher he had ever had and that Diana had just gotten saved that weekend, we would have hesitated about letting them come.

But we didn't know, and off they went to Guatemala for the summer. To our amazement, they both blossomed during the trip, and God began an incredible transformation in their lives. As they reached out to share the Lord with the nationals, I could see their faith coming alive inside them. I saw them embrace a personal relationship with Jesus. It was no longer their parents' religion — Jesus became real to them!

I remember watching Jeremy "bringing in the net" after we presented a drama in a market. ("Bringing in the net" is the phrase Teen Mania uses for an altar call.) He was telling the crowd how to have a relationship with Christ when, in the middle of his mini-sermon, he just stopped talking. All of a sudden this fourteen-year-old church-wise kid was overcome with compassion for the people. He began to cry. "I just want you to know that I love you. Jesus loves you. He gave His life for you. I love you. I really love you," he kept saying over and over with tears rolling down his cheeks.

These two were radically changed by the Lord, and it did not go unnoticed by their peers and family when they returned home. Jeremy confessed to his parents that he had been cheating on tests in school for as long as he could remember, and he wanted to make it right. His parents started tutoring him, and, although his grades dropped a little, he gradually improved and is now attending a university.

After returning from the mission field, these two young people were obsessed with telling their youth group and friends about what happened in their lives while they were overseas. They went to various youth groups around their area to share their story and invite more youth to come overseas the next year. As a result of their fire, sixteen young people accompanied them on the mission trip the next year.

When the group returned, something began to shake in the state of Maryland. These sixteen went back to their various schools and churches and talked about how God had changed their lives. I heard about parents who had rededicated their lives to the Lord as a result of their kids' lives being changed. What followed was nothing short of a sovereign move of God. Over the next few years, 26 teens went on the missions trip, then 52, 86 and finally 110! The teens came from many different types of churches. They were from a wide variety of schools and socioeconomic back-grounds. I heard not only of parents being changed when their kids returned home, but of whole churches breaking out in revival!

Parents who renewed their commitments or made first-time commitments to the Lord started going to church. A season of renewal penetrated the Northeast in over forty different churches because of the witness of teenagers.

James Sturrock

James was a fairly new Christian when he first came on a summer missions trip with Teen Mania. He em-barked on one of the most grueling mission endeavors we had ever proposed — a trip to Nicaragua. The intensity of the trip changed James forever. He re-turned home with an incredible seriousness about his faith and his purpose in life. A junior in high school, he shared his faith freely and in a relatable manner with his friends at school.

Little did he know what was about to happen. One day two of the players on the high school football team got into trouble with their parents and were forbidden to leave their homes for any reason. Desper-ate to get out of their houses, they asked their parents if they could leave to attend a Bible study. Their parents agreed. Now all they had to do was find one.

Their first thought was to call James because he was the known Christian at school. So one of the football players called him on the phone and said, "James, will you lead a Bible study with me and a few of the guys?"

James was blown away. Is this some kind of joke? he thought.

Then the football player explained that a Bible study was the only way he and his friends could get out of their houses, but James agreed to do it anyway.

That first night James had prayed up and was prepared for God to move in the lives of these muscle-bound heathens. About thirty football players and their friends showed up that night. As he shared his passion for Christ with conviction, James got through to these rugged peers. He presented them with the reality of a relationship with Jesus. They had come for a good time, but they got a lot more than they bargained for. By the end of the night every person was on his face, weeping before God and committing his life to Him!

The other students heard about what had happened and were curious. In the following weeks, dozens of others came to the Bible study by invitation or just out of curiosity. By the end of the year, more than three hundred had visited or were coming to the Bible study on a weekly basis.

James continued to grow as a leader. During his senior year, when he was only seventeen years old, he was asked to be a youth pastor at a local church. As of this writing he is overseas working as a missionary.

Ana Bonafede

Only a year ago Ana was just another teenager at school, an average sixteen-year-old but a good churchgoer. Ana had heard it all before but never really embraced the power of a radical Christian life for herself. Then it happened.

When she signed up for the conference, she thought she was just going along for another youth activity with all her friends. They expected to have fun during their free time at the convention. But that weekend at the Acquire the Fire Convention would make her a radical forever. She had an encounter with the living God that she could not keep to herself.

She went home and started a Bible club in her school. She reached out to her friends, and they reached out to others. The Bible club now numbers over one hundred participants each week. She keeps the Bible study lively by allowing discussion, and she uses the Acquire the Fire leadership guide that we provide for youth pastors.

Frank Jenson

Frank was probably considered a little less than average when he first came on a Teen Mania missions trip. We didn't know that he had been kicked out of several schools because of his attitude and was on probation at his present school because of his poor grades.

He had become discouraged during his preparation time for the mission field. His money came in slowly. He was about to give up, but his mother would not let him. (Thank God for mothers like this!) She challenged him, "God would not have given you this much money so far if He did not want you to go."

Finally he got dismissed from high school for his grades. That was it. It was more than Frank could take. He decided not to go. But his mother prevailed. They got the rest of the money, and he was on his way.

During the course of the trip, Frank seemed to be a fairly normal teen. Nothing would have indicated that he had endured these kinds of tough times at school and home. That is exactly how it is with most teens.

*A crowd of teens may appear
to be their normal, wild
selves when their hearts
are full of pain.*

One day the entire team decided to hike up a volcano for a free-day activity. It is incredible the things you can do when in another country. The deal was that every one of the team members had to make it to the top or the whole group would stop. It put pressure on the team to work together and on the individuals to push themselves.

Frank was having a really hard time making it to the top. It was windy and cold. He was tired and hungry and could not think of one good reason to go all the way to the top. He wondered why he had even come on this mission trip. He wished he could go home early. He complained to himself and God as he climbed.

About halfway up, he felt like sitting down and giving up on everything. He was in pain and completely exhausted. He had failed at everything else — what was one more failure? As he complained to God, something incredible happened. As he tells it:

"God spoke to me so clearly. He said, 'If you make it to the top of that mountain, there is nothing that you can't do!'"

All of a sudden a surge of energy came over him. He climbed harder and faster up the mountain than he had all day. He had a determination to make it to the top. And he did. It was a triumphant moment in his life — he could be a winner!

A few months later I went to preach in his home church. His mother came up and grabbed my arm and told me the story you just read. Her tears washed the makeup from her eyes as she said that Frank was now back home, in school and on the dean's honor list. Frank is a real-life world-changer.

PART FIVE

WHERE DO WE GO FROM HERE?

So far we have examined the current
situation of the teens sitting in the pews of our
churches. They have plenty of knowledge but
lack fire and passion for God. We have discussed
the events that brought us to this point and our
need to see this generation in a new light.
But as you can see from the last chapter, in the
midst of all this turmoil God is doing some
awesome things among our teens.
Now what should we do?
What is our response? How can we see vast
numbers of our teens *acquire* the fire that
some have discovered? What are the vital
ingredients of our responsibility to
inspire the fire and keep it going
in our young people? How do we keep
it going in our own lives?

FOURTEEN

PREVENTIVE MEDICINE

IN SPITE OF all the symptoms affecting this troubled generation, we can see some signs of hope. But still you may ask, "What can I do to keep my kids from falling into the apathy trap?"

I know that no well-meaning Christian parent wants his or her teen to get duped into an experience of monotonous Christianity. Just as no well-meaning parent wants his or her kid to experience drinking, drug abuse or teenage pregnancy. The puzzle is: If so many do not want it to happen, why does it happen so often?

It is not enough to be a well-meaning parent — good intentions are not enough. We've got to move from intentions to responsibilities. If we relinquish our responsibilities to the electronic baby-sitter, we will end up with a member of the MTV generation living in our home.

The cry of the parent of every average teen in the American church is this: "I raised my teen in the church all his life — why is he like this?"

How have we let society influence our teens more than the church, the Bible or our own lives? It's as though they were kidnapped and brainwashed while living in our homes. Our young people have been taken captive right under our noses.

The Quiet Killer

Apathy. It has infected our youth and spread like gangrene. It is an epidemic that no one knows how to fight. *Webster's* dictionary defines apathy as "lack of emotion, lack of interest, a listless condition, uncon- cern, indifference." This could also accurately de- scribe the average Christian school or youth group.

If we are such godly parents, why has apathy crept into our kids' lives? Are we doing something wrong?

As Christian parents we ought to be the role models for the world — their example of parenting. People in the world ought to say, "Could my family be like that if I became a Christian?"

Instead, many times we are the ones taking our kids to counselors and specialists provided by the world to get advice for our teens. The religious group renowned for positive family life is not the average Christians — it's the Mormons. They stole the principles from us and packaged them with a false theology. Now the Mormon church attracts many people under the guise of having a "good family life." It is time we recapture the reputation of a quality home life and recapture the hearts and minds of our kids.

Relationship — the Key

We are engaged in an offensive battle for our youth. It is up to us — the parents — to reassemble our dissolving family lives. We must deal with our fragmented families and the busy schedules that push us further and further apart.

We cannot hope to influence our kids if we are hardly ever with them.

Instead of running in a thousand different directions, learn to be involved in your loved ones' lives. Appreciate each other's interests. Our selfish human nature makes it easy to believe that my interests are the most important thing. We become self-absorbed in whatever activity suits our fancy, often to the exclusion of our own children.

Establishing and maintaining a relationship with your young people will be an incredible bridge in communicating your Christian values to them.

Let me clarify. Establishing a close-bonded relationship, by our teens' definition, is the key. Many parents think they are close to their teens, but if you ask the teens it's a different story. In reality, most parents don't have a clue what is going on in their teens' minds and hearts. Would *your* teens consider you close? Would they consider you one of their best friends?

We polled the parents of teens who had participated in Teen Mania and asked them about their relationship with their children. Almost all of them (97 percent) said they felt close to their kids, and many (87 percent) said they were closer to their kids than their parents were to them.[1]

That is great, but what do the kids think? We often think we know our kids and believe ourselves to be relatable, while actually we are living in our own make-believe world. That is why so many parents are shocked or go into denial when informed that their child is doing drugs or is pregnant out of wedlock. "Surely not my child!"

We do not know them as we think we do.

Here's a quiz to see how well you know your son or daughter.

- How do your teens feel about current issues?

- How are they doing in every class at school?

- What do they worry about most?

- What are their greatest fears?

- What are their greatest struggles in life?

- Who are their best friends?

- What do they aspire to do with their lives?

- What are their wildest dreams?

- How have they been hurt in life?

- Whom do they tell their secrets to?

- How well do you know them?

Our preaching to them rolls off their backs like water off a duck. Without the strength of a relationship, they have no incentive to listen. They feel as if you want to influence their lives but have no genuine interest in what is really going on with them. And we, in turn, diagnose this as a hard heart.

Communication Begins With Listening

Listening to others is something most people do not do well. Sure, they have conversations, but they walk away satisfied only if they made their own point clear. We often do not listen while the other person is talking. We are thinking about what we are going to say when they quit talking — or thinking about who is going to win the Super Bowl, or what we are going to do that day, or how we can win the argument. As soon as they pause for half a second to take a breath, we shoot in our side of the argument.

Our kids have learned a lot from us when it comes to listening, so they are treating us the same way. Our conversations sound more like verbal wrestling matches than a sharing of hearts. Did you ever walk away from a conversation wondering why you didn't get through to your teen? The answer is simple: You didn't.

If we want to be understood, we must seek to understand first. Proverbs 1:5 says that "the wise listen and add to their learning." Do you want to be wise? Listen to your kids. Really tune in to them. Find out what they are feeling. You might think, What could I possibly learn from my teen? Your teens have already guessed that's what you think, and that is why they won't share their hearts with you.

You would be amazed at what you can learn from your own kids. If nothing else, you will learn what a sixteen-year-old thinks about life in the nineties. Volumes are still to be written on that subject.

Proverbs also says, "He who answers before listening — that is his folly and his shame" (18:13). Many parents have fulfilled this and do not even know it.

If we do not listen to our kids, they will find someone who will. It may be a grandparent, aunt or uncle. Or it may be the rebellious kids at school or the cynical Christians that make fun of the preacher. MTV says the reason they are so successful is because they listen to our kids.

Something happens when you listen. The person sees that you think he is important enough to tune into. As a result, his heart is drawn toward you. He knows that you are taking time to listen to what he thinks. He also becomes more willing to listen to you, since you listened first.

When we share our faith, we should start by asking questions and listening. "What do you think about

God?" and "How do you think someone can go to heaven?" are great ways to begin a conversation. After they have shared their perspective with you, they will be a lot more willing to listen to yours.

One good way to tune into your teens is to force yourself to repeat in your mind what they just said. Focus on it. It will keep your mind from wandering off to the World Series or the mall. When parents tell me, "I don't know why there is a wall between my kids and me. How did it get there?" I ask, "When did you stop listening to your kids?" If we would just stop talking and begin listening, we could draw their hearts back toward us and re-establish a strong relationship with them.

You will be amazed at how they listen to you when you take the time to listen to them.

Learning to Share Our Hearts

In John 15 Jesus shared with His disciples the fact that He wanted to change the kind of relationship He had with them. He wanted them to be friends — not just servants (John 15:15).

At some point our relationship with our teens must evolve into friendship. It would be cruel to think, I like having my kids serve me. In fact, the reason I had them is so I wouldn't have to mow the lawn and do the dishes anymore.

Being a good parent involves more than providing a roof over the head and food for the belly. Countless parents tell their children, "Look at all we have given you!" They are expecting that to be enough reason for them to obey. Well, Jesus did a lot for His disciples too. But He took the leap to transform His relationship with them into a friendship. Can we do any less with our own teens?

In John 15:15 Jesus said, "I no longer call you servants, because a servant does not know his master's business. Instead, I have called you friends, for everything that I learned from My Father I have made known to you."

Jesus shared things with His disciples — His friends — that He would tell to no one else. It was as if He said, "I am sharing with you what My Father has told Me about the end times. I share with you what He has said about your ministry. I tell everyone the parables, but I tell you their meaning. You know My heart. You know what is really going on inside Me. You know what I am made of. You really know Me — you're My friends!"

The pivotal word in John 15:15 is the word *for*. Jesus was declaring them His friends because of what He was about to say. What qualified them to be His friends was the fact that He had shared His heart with them. He let them in on things He would tell no one else.

Do you want to develop a friendship with your kids? Share your heart with them. Talk to them.

This does not mean the usual telling them what to do or discussing the household chores. Share a little bit of what is going on inside of you. Share some of your struggles. Talk about some of your victories. Tell them about challenges you faced when you were their age. I am not talking about the stories of how you "walked to school every day barefoot in the snow." They have already heard those stories. Share how you felt during times of difficulty and times of really doing well.

Maybe you feel, "My kids don't need to know my business."

They do not want to know your business. They want to know you.

When I was a teen, a friend told me, "My dad is my best friend. I can tell him anything." I remember thinking, I wish I could tell my dad anything. There is a part inside your young person that longs for a friendship with Mom and Dad. Without the element of friendship, he or she will feel distanced from you. As you share your heart with them, you will find that they will also be much more willing to share their hearts with you.

It is not enough to communicate household duties and schedules. Such households are filled with strangers who do not know each other. Friendships are built as people share their hearts with each other.

Out of the Mouth of Babes

We have gained valuable insights from the surveys we have administered to teens across North America. Look at the answers we got when we asked them to complete the following statement: "I would really want to go after God for myself if my parents would just stop..."

- bugging me

- acting like hypocrites

- pushing me hard

- yelling at me

- forcing me to do what they want me to do

- bringing up my past mistakes

- pressuring me

- refusing to let me go at my own pace

- nagging me

- getting on my case

- fighting

- lecturing me

- preaching at me

It is easy to believe we are trying to get through to our kids while all the time doing things that negate the relationship we have with them.

Although we may try desperately to get through to them about spiritual things, we must have an incredibly close relationship with them to be able to do it. It is a paradox. At times the very things that we do to try to get through may put up walls in our relationship with them. Thus we end up with a greater distance between us than what we started with.

We also asked young people this question: "What one thing have your parents done to help in your walk with the Lord?" Here are some of their responses:

- My mom has raised me in faith since birth and has continually prayed for me.

- They have been an excellent example.

- My parents have a weekly Bible study, go to church and live it!

- They have taught me to have a prayer time.

- My parents took me to church when I didn't want to go.

- They ask me what's wrong when they know I'm not doing well.

- They let me go on mission trips.

- Mom and Dad put me in a Christian school.

- My mom and I are starting to read the Bible every night.

- Mom and Dad always stick by me.

- They have encouraged me to be radical with God and do everything I can to get closer to God.

- My parents corrected me when I was wrong.

- They let me go on retreats and to all the youth functions.

- My mom has invited me to church events with her.

- They don't overcrowd me.

- They let me come to Acquire the Fire.

- They've always been there for me.

When we asked parents what were some of the most successful things they had done to reach their teens, they responded:

- Sharing with him and listening to him.

- Letting the Spirit lead me in what I say to her.

- Youth retreats and youth group.

- Telling her I was wrong.

- Leaving her alone and letting her make up her own mind.

- Reading the Bible with her.

- Christian school, hugs, telling them we love them — being consistent in discipline.

- Living a Christian walk.

- Not pushing, but guiding.

- Heart-to-heart talks about a life without Christ versus a life with Christ.

- Spiritual warfare, Teen Mania, camp.

- Having missionaries in our home, going on mission trips, conferences, going on dates with them.

How do you know if you are in touch with your teens or not? What were your answers to the quiz I gave you earlier regarding how well you know your kids? If you can answer these and other questions, you are on the way to getting to know your teen.

Establish good communication habits while they are young. Then continue them as they become adolescents. It becomes harder as they grow older because so many other things are competing for their attention and time. It takes work as a parent to stay in touch with your teens. Get acquainted with their friends, listen to their music and be aware of what they think is cool. You have to seek out this information — it is a continuous research project.

The mark of a good missionary is that he keeps learning. You are like a missionary to your teen. You are trying to reach him. It is not easy, but it is possible.

As you shore up and solidify the stability of your relationship with your teen, you will find that communicating your passion for God will be natural for you. You will no longer have to preach to them. They will see a glimpse of what is in your heart just as Jesus' disciples did with Him. When they see that, you will have successfully given them the best heritage of all.

FIFTEEN

SETTING UP AN ENCOUNTER WITH GOD

IN THE MIDST of preparing to write this chapter, God had His own way of preparing me. I have prayed for it, dreamed about it, longed for it and read about it from days of old. But when it happens, it almost seems too good to be true. But it does happen, and I feel so inadequate to put it into words.

It all started as we were preparing for the Saturday

night session of our Acquire the Fire convention in Nashville. Everything seemed pretty normal except for an extraordinary amount of technical problems throughout the weekend. A great expectancy had filled me as I came into the weekend — God was going to do something great. But I could not have imagined what was about to happen.

I encouraged our staff and team to pray earnestly for a "great move of God." I wanted our prayers to be more than just habitual rhetoric.

The crowd of twenty-five hundred teens and leaders seemed a little more rowdy than the usual Saturday crowd. It would be a challenge to funnel all that energy into seeking the Lord. We started the service with four or five fast praise songs, being careful to give all the glory to Jesus.

I led them into singing a few slower worship songs, and that's when it began to happen. The teens took ownership of each of the songs we sang. They personalized them, and an earnestness rang loud in the room. For a long time after each worship song, the kids sang a *new song,* making up words from their own hearts to the Lord. Even though I was trying to be careful not to drag the service on, they were unwilling to move quickly through the worship.

Spontaneous applause broke out after each song — uncoerced. Again and again they waited for me to lead them in another worship song, and I did. Again...and again...and again. It was as if they would not let me quit.

Hey, who is in charge of this meeting anyway? Me or them?...Or God?

145

I gave an altar call for those who felt they were not really committed to Jesus Christ. I invited those who had been running from Him to give their all to Him. Although this altar call came after an entire weekend of ministry, where hundreds had already answered a previous altar call, the kids came from all over the auditorium. They jammed the front altar space and stretched all the way back down the aisles. Three or four hundred kids had streamed to the altar to get right with God in the middle of worship!

We continued to worship after we prayed. One hour and fifteen minutes later I decided to end the worship service in order to get focused on the rest of the service. But the kids were still on their faces! Hundreds — all over the auditorium — were weeping, some kneeling, others standing with hands raised. I asked them to return to their seats, but some were oblivious to my request. It was becoming obvious that God had a different program in mind.

Someone yelled "Jesus!" and spontaneous applause erupted. Knowing the propensity that teens have for hype, I was skeptical, so I tried to focus their attention on the next portion of the service. But we had just experienced a few moments in the throne room, and no one wanted to leave. The crowd seemed to be asking, "Why are we rushing out of God's presence?"

"It doesn't have to stop now — it can go on tomorrow, the next day, next week and next month," I commented. Though they all applauded, my words did not seem to satisfy them. Something was stirring in them, and I was trying to discover the validity of it. Some sat down as I requested them to do so for the second time, but many shouted with a genuine thunder of praise and joy. The rest jumped to their feet to join them.

As they finally quieted down, I said, "When you get into the presence of God, you don't need to preach your little sermons — God can preach His own sermon." I realized that I was talking to myself, and God wasn't interested in *my* little sermon that night either. Their ovation seemed endless. I mentioned that we needed to get free of our schedules and programs from time to time to let God move, and they erupted again.

The next hour was one of the most incredible experiences of my life. They had barely calmed down when on one side of the auditorium a small group started chanting, "J.C...J.C...J.C!" In moments, the whole crowd was yelling it as fervently as they could. After a few minutes of that, a deafening shout of joy rang out for several more minutes. This happened over and over again.

It was as if they were in the presence of a great hero. No one wanted to leave, and no one knew what to do.

Their only response was to continue cheering Him out of the gratefulness of their overflowing hearts.

I really didn't know what to do. Didn't they know I had a strict schedule to follow? Didn't they know I had a whole program for the evening?

In the middle of all this I was trying to distinguish hype from a sincere move of the Almighty. But no one was bringing glory or attention to himself. That was a good sign, but I wondered how to take back control of the meeting. Or even if I should.

*I had been praying for a move of
God upon the teens like this for years.
Now that it was actually happening
before my eyes, did I dare
consider shutting it down?*

I looked at the agenda to see what I could eliminate from the program and realized the first thing to go would be the video we had planned.

During the course of any convention we show several videos, perform skits and occasionally spice things up with controlled pyrotechnic bombs and fire displays. We do this with a monster equipment setup including floor-to-ceiling video walls, light shows with robotic lights, cameras for instant magnification and a full-blown sound system. All of this is designed to reiterate points that I make in my sermons.

But I realized God had no need of that Christian high-tech bonanza on that evening. He had His own way of getting His point across.

I eliminated more of my planned schedule of events. Next to go was the skits. I glanced at the manual I use to preach from and realized it was futile to try to go along with any of our planned agenda. God had commandeered the ship. I was just along for the ride.

Thoughts crowded into my mind: How far should I let this go? Is this just a bunch of teenage hype? Was I letting the teens run the meeting, or was God doing something sovereign? If God had planned this in advance, why didn't He let me know? I remembered the unusual feeling of expectancy I had experienced before the weekend, but who expected this?

I decided to flow with it instead of fight it. As I read one of the Scripture passages I had planned for the evening, the celebration began again. I tried to share from my heart about the destiny God has for their generation. When I said, "God wants to use you to change the world," they could not contain themselves.

I reasoned with them, "God has visited you in such a great way because He wants you to take it to the world." I described people around the world who were crying out, "God, if You are really there, please send someone to tell us how to find You!" I explained that not many were willing to go.

Suddenly I heard a very soft chant begin somewhere in the auditorium. As the rest of the teens joined in, I understood their words: "We will go. We will go." An overwhelming echo filled the room. Every single person in the room was involved in what God was doing that night. There were no onlookers — no one could deny we were in the midst of our encounter with the Most High.

As I reflect back on that awesome move of God, I wonder what historical significance that night may have. It was an experience that neither I nor any of the teens will ever forget.

I don't have experiences like that every day or even every year. But it drove home a point to me: God is sovereign. He moves with us and despite us. That's a key concept for anyone who wants to bring people closer to God.

The Goal of the Ministry

When I went to college, I was startled to discover

there was a lot more to ministry than preaching. I just wanted to stand behind a pulpit and preach my heart out all my life. I learned about organizing, planning, administrating, accounting and printing — plus maintaining an office. The list seemed to go on and on. This was all necessary in order to give the pastor an opportunity to preach once or twice a week. It seemed like a lot of work to get to do what you really loved for two hours a week.

A friend of mine shared with me a principle that has stuck with me through all my training and ministry. "All of this work," he explained, "is designed to organize the logistics so the people can be at the right place at the right time to hear from God." Basically everything we call "the work of the ministry" is simply setting up an encounter with God.

We, as ministers and parents, are trying to give people the opportunity to get their hearts in the right condition to hear from the Lord.

The problem is that most people get so preoccupied with the work of setting up the opportunity that they forget the goal was to give God a chance to move.

We start thinking the goal is to work out all the logistics. As long as the offering is taken at the right time, the choir sings on schedule and no one misses his cue, we think we are successful.

Even in our personal walk with the Lord, this tendency rules our lives. As long as we read a certain amount of the Bible each week (or year), we feel pretty good about our Christian life. As long as we pray regularly (or semi-regularly), we have confidence in our spiritual stability. We concentrate on the mechanics of what it takes to have a good Christian life instead of on the goal of those mechanics: an intimate encounter with the Most High on a regular basis.

We say we have a personal relationship with Christ and that He is our friend. Unfortunately, this is just rhetoric for many Christians. The personal closeness of God's presence seems like a mystery to most.

They Were Singing to Someone

For most of my life I was raised in church. I heard about God at Sunday school, church and vacation Bible school on a regular basis. I heard the words "personal relationship with Christ" my whole life but never understood what they meant. I had even made a commitment to Christ when I was twelve, but I had never encountered the presence of God.

My salvation was a cerebral experience — the mental assent to believe the right things. I believed in a personal relationship with Jesus; but if it were so personal, why didn't I sense a closeness with God?

Then a friend of mine named Mike invited me to his church. I was sixteen years old and in the midst of my rebellious drug and alcohol days. I enjoyed my new-found popularity among the druggies at school. When Mike showed up to take me to church, I was still sleeping. He waited while I got ready, and off we went.

The service had already started when we walked into the church. I tried to sing along with the others, but something seemed different. I had been to many churches before, but I never had heard people singing like this. It was as if they were singing *to someone*. Who could it be? I looked all over the stage to see who they were serenading. Then I heard some of the words of the songs.

They were singing songs to Jesus as if He could hear them.

They were singing love songs to Him. I felt a warmth come over me unlike any I had ever felt before. All of my attention had been drawn to Him. It dawned on me that He was real! I had been in church my whole life, yet it had never occurred to me before that God was real. I began to sing to Him myself and could not believe the sense of closeness to Him I felt.

God stopped me in the middle of the worst case of teenage rebellion I could imagine and got my attention. No one told me to give my life to Jesus that day at church. I just did it because I knew He was real. And because He was real, I thought I had no option but to live for Him. No one told me to stop drinking and doing drugs — I just stopped. God was real, and that was all that mattered.

What Is the Answer?

People have many opinions about how to solve the problems of the nineties. We are overwhelmed with teenage pregnancy, drug abuse and gun-toting rebels in the high schools who put fear in the average American.

Some say peer counseling is the answer. Others think getting involved in social services is the solution. Others say that "just say no" will work. More are convinced that some kind of professional therapy is the answer. In-patient psychiatric care facilities are a booming industry especially designed for the parent who cannot figure out what to do with a problem teen. It's a high-priced baby-sitter approach for the beleaguered parent. But many of these solutions don't make any real change in the kid's life.

The answer for these teens is not in modern adolescent psychology. They do not need just another counseling session.

They need an encounter with the living God!

When you get close to the real thing, He has a way of reducing the problems to nothing. This generation has been abused, hurt, neglected, cut off and stomped on. I have personally hugged the necks of hundreds of sobbing teenage guys and girls who have been ripped off by the circumstances of this life. No surgeon can perform the kind of surgery needed to put these hearts back together. There is only one person who can heal those kinds of hurts. Only a tangible encounter with the great I AM can restore this generation.

These young people need a "Saul on the road to Damascus" experience (see Acts 9). God has a way of silencing every mocker. He has a way of getting through when everything we have tried has failed.

Principles That Bring This Encounter

There are no magic words and no special formulas

that make it all happen the way we want every time. An encounter with God won't come by repeating a ritual.

Humans are famous for taking true experience — like an encounter with God — and turning it into vain tradition hoping to conjure up His presence again. We think if we just sing the same song enough times, He will manifest Himself because He did the last time we sang it.

God will not be harnessed by our trite spiritual motions. Instead, He has given us principles in the Bible that we can follow to get our hearts in the right condition to receive Him when He does show up.

At the risk of someone's turning these into another ritual, I will share what I have found to be true. We can use these in the context of our own quiet times with God or incorporate them into how we minister to our teenage children or youth group.

Repentance

The first step in getting through to the presence of God is to *ask Him to show you the sin in your life that He wants you to get rid of.* When you ask this question, it is amazing how the floodgates of heaven will be opened as He speaks. He always wants to speak to us — we are just asking the wrong questions. There are areas in our lives that He wants to clean up and make more like Himself. Ask Him what they are. You will be astounded by the clarity of His answer.

After David's sin of adultery with Bathsheba, he cried out, "Create in me a pure heart, O God, and renew a steadfast spirit within me. Do not cast me from your presence or take your Holy Spirit from me" (Ps. 51:10-11). He knew the sin would push him away from God's presence, so he was determined to get rid of it.

A Genuine Spirit of Worship

We must have a *genuine spirit of worship*. The Bible says God "inhabit[s] the praises of His people" (Ps. 22:3, KJV). God inhabited our praises in the service in Nashville that I mentioned earlier. When God starts to inhabit something, everyone knows it. Psalm 100:4 says, "Enter His gates with thanksgiving and His courts with praise." If we want to get in there with Him, we must worship Him with all our hearts.

I am not talking about the canned worship tunes that we sing over and over again until they lose their meaning. I am talking about singing with all our hearts, letting Him know that we truly honor Him.

We need some fresh creativity in our worship. Look at the Psalms. David was very creative. In fact, you could read the Psalms to the Lord as if they were directly from you. Look at the creative ways David worshipped God. Worshipping is not just singing the songs from a hymnal or overhead projector. It is letting those words flow from your heart to His. This is the worship that will usher you into the courts of the Most High.

Get Real With God

Simply put, the third step is to *get real with God*. He does not want a ritualistic prayer time. Pour out your heart and soul to Him. Talk to Him about what is really going on in your life.

Jeremiah 29:13 says, "You will seek me and find me when you seek me with *all your heart*" (italics added). Some people go through the motions of seeking God but find nothing because they are not seeking Him with all their hearts. Churches are filled with people like this, and they wonder why God never seems to show up. He promises *you will find Him* when you get honest and seek Him with all your heart.

A Desperate Desire

Finally, there must be a *desperation about our desire to find Him.* Do we seek Him casually, or are we laying it all on the line? David says, "As the deer pants for streams of water, so my soul pants for you, O God" (Ps. 42:1). That deer is desperate. How desperate are you? How badly do you thirst? Are you ready and willing to do whatever it takes to get that water?

As parents and leaders, our job is to set up and provide for an ongoing environment where this can happen for our teens. The ideal is to woo them to a place where they have that desire for themselves. As we inspire them with the possibility of an encounter with God and let them see that we are seeking God with all our hearts, we will lead them to the answer they long for — an encounter with the living God.

SIXTEEN

PROVIDING THE OPPORTUNITY

As CHRISTIAN PARENTS and leaders, we want our teens to be radical for Christ. Our pleas have become a routine part of our repertoire of important things to say.

Even most teens will tell you that they know they should be radical. But they also have a glaring awareness that they don't know what to do to be radical. We tell them *what* to do without telling them *how* to do it.

They jam the altars to give their all to God. But after a few weeks go by, they end up with the same condition of heart they had before they responded. The common thought of disillusioned teens is, Forget it. I just can't do it.

We, as leaders and parents, must provide a specific road map showing them *how* to get to where we are asking them to go. I am not talking about organizing several more youth activities for your kids. Far be it from me to busy up the schedule of already frazzled parents and teens. I am not implying you should give them more things to do just to keep them occupied. We have plenty of those things already. We do not need to provide a multitude of Christian social activities to keep them from getting into trouble.

We need to give them
assertive directives that will
cause them to make a deadly
assault on the kingdom
of darkness.

Moses Is the Man

A glance back at Moses and his youth group shows us how he covered his bases. As he tried to get the children of Israel to understand *who* they were in God's plan, he gave them directives to help them understand what kind of people they should be.

If You Do Not Give Them Something to Do, They Will Find Something on Their Own

Remember when Moses went up the mountain and was gone for forty days? What did the Israelites do? They built an altar out of gold in the shape of a calf. They had just been delivered by the awesome living God — they had just walked through the Red Sea. Now they were bowing down before a piece of gold (see Ex. 32).

When you look at this story, maybe your teen does not look so bad after all. The principle is this: If you do not give them something to do, they will find something on their own.

What did Moses do? He went back up the mountain and got something for them to do. He came down with the plan to build the tabernacle. He put everyone to work. He got their energy working for him and not against him. He *provided an opportunity* for them to do something practical to reach their goals.

Everyone had something to do. He had some cut the wood. He had others work with the precious metals. Still others wove the linens and engraved the utensils. *Everyone* was asked to give willingly of his gold, silver and goods to make the project happen (see Ex. 35). People ended up giving more than Moses could even use. He had to ask them to quit giving (Ex. 36:6-7).

There is a desire in the heart of every teen to give himself *and* his stuff (money) once he sees a specific cause worthy of his all.

As the Israelites poured themselves and their time into building the tabernacle and the ark of the covenant, they discovered more of their identity. As they realized they were working for the almighty God, a sense of holy pride took root in them as a people.

Jesus' Marching Orders

Often people get so caught up in the inward walk of their faith that they forget there is an outer adventure to be had. There is something we must do. There is a world to be won. Strategies must be made. Risks must be taken. It is not just a casual inner growth that God has in mind. In fact, I have heard Christian leaders say that some people's Christianity looks a lot like Buddhism. They are referring to Christians who are completely preoccupied with the inner journey and think that is all there is to the Christian life.

Jesus was interested in both. We have already examined how He constantly pumped vision into His disciples to change the world. He did not stop there, however. He took them with Him on His ministry outings. He wanted them to see how it was done. He wanted them to be there as God used Him so they could do the same things and be used in the same way.

Right after Jesus told the disciples to pray that the Lord of the harvest would send out laborers into the field, He told them to go (Luke 10:2-3). He wanted them to be part of the answer to their own prayer. He wanted them to be part of the adventure too. They were not to stand idly by and watch Him do everything. He wanted them to take an active part.

Many young people are bored with their limited awareness of what God offers in the Christian life.

Jesus got His disciples involved with the supernatural, and they were never bored with it.

Too Young to Be Used?

Jesus said, "Go! I am sending you out like lambs among wolves" (Luke 10:3). He was pointing out, "I am sending you out when you are young. You are all lambs. You are not even sheep yet."

Jesus gave them an opportunity to do something historic, something supernatural.

Many parents think, How could I let my kids go on a mission trip? They are too young. Then they concede, Well, I guess God can use them even though they are young. Notice that Jesus did not say He would use them in spite of the fact that they were young. I believe He uses youth because of the fact that they are young. They are versatile, they have no long-term commitments, and they have lots of energy.

In verse 17 the disciples came back excited that they had seen miracles and that God had really used them. Jesus did not need to razzle-dazzle them from the outside. He stimulated their hearts with the Spirit of God as He used them to change people's lives.

It reminds me of the fire I have seen in thousands of teenagers' lives who have gone overseas on mission trips. God uses them, and they are never the same.

Later Jesus sent the disciples out again. The first trip was not just a one-time adventure. He wanted it to be a habit, a lifestyle. This time He sent out seventy-two to go to the surrounding villages with the message and power of God. He was showing them there is an outward adventure to have in this Christian life. It has to do with changing the world!

Ultimately He sent them out and told them never to come back. The Great Commission in Matthew 28 was not the great suggestion. It was and is an imperative. It was essential not only to reach the world but to sustain the fire in their lives.

> Therefore go and make disciples of all nations, baptizing them in the name of the Father and of the Son and of the Holy Spirit, and teaching them to obey everything I have commanded you. And surely I will be with you always, to the very end of the age (Matt. 28:19-20).

If we are going to *inspire the fire* of God in our kids' lives, we must give them the opportunity to get the fire as Jesus let His disciples get it.

Now is the time for us to give our teens something to do that will push them onto the radical edge for God. Many young people have told me of the frustration they felt when they told their Christian parents they wanted to go on a mission trip, and their parents responded with a firm no. These young people are having to fight to fulfill the destiny on their lives!

I have talked to many teens who have the desire to go on a mission trip but have been forbidden by their parents. They want so badly to go and be used by God but have had to wait. Some parents have prayed,

"Lord, please don't make my kid a missionary. I want him to be a success in life."

We say we want our kids to do great things for God, but when the rubber meets the road it is harder than we thought it would be to let go. This is the plight of every parent who has ever had one of his children change the world.

Parents ask me, "How old should my child be before I let him go on a mission trip?" We start taking teens when they are thirteen and a half because we have seen the effects on their lives if they start while they are young. If they have the desire to go while they are young, let them go!

Some well-meaning parents say, "We are going to wait until he is sixteen to let him go." The problem is that you do not know if he will still want to go at that age. We have found that the older they get, the more distracted they can become with getting a job, having their own money and doing other "adult things." Thank God that they want to go at all! Let them go while they have the desire!

I have had many parents thank me for taking their teens overseas once the parents saw the change when they returned. I remember one man who told me he thought I was crazy for wanting to take his daughter to Russia. He thought it was even crazier that she wanted to go. He decided that if God wanted her to go, He would supply the money.

She ended up going, and the father thought the trip would never be over. He related how hard it was to think of his baby all the way around the world. When she returned, she was filled with great testimonies of how God had used her to reach the Russian people.

With tears running down his face, he said to me, "When I saw the video of my baby passing out tracts to those Russian people, I knew it had all been worth it!"

Let us not be the ones to keep our youth from fulfilling their call!

We should be catalysts for their call. Help them pack their bags. Consider it an honor that God wants to use your teen. Thank God that He put that desire in your teen in the first place. You know it must be God, because in the midst of this selfish "me generation," only God could make a teen want to give away his summer.

SEVENTEEN

LIVING A RADICAL EXAMPLE

WE HAVE EXAMINED the plight of teen-age churched America, but we have also seen a glimpse of the destiny for this generation. There are great signs of hope in the young people of today.

As parents and leaders, we are coming to grips with our role in releasing the potential of this generation. We are planting the gospel in their hearts and believing in their potential. The question that awaits us now is this:

Are we just going to tell them what to do, or are we going to show them?

Ask yourself: Am I the kind of person I would want my kids to model themselves after? Or was it the *me of the past* that I want them to be like?

Answer these questions honestly: If my kids knew everything about my life, would they still want to follow me? Is there anything I am ashamed for them to know about me?

Don't Do What I Do?

We have all heard someone say in a sermon at some point, "Now I'm preaching to myself here too, folks. I'm not just talking to you, but also to yours truly." Although this sounds like a mark of humility, it is also communicating something very hazardous to the crowd.

When I hear someone say that, I think, So, wait a minute. Although you are admitting you have not figured out how to do this, still you want me to do it? You go and figure out how and start doing it. Then come and tell me how you did it.

When we ask someone to do something that we are not doing, we never carry the authority that will convince them to do it. We are not even convinced ourselves that it is possible, so how can we convince others it is? There is no conviction in our communication.

Many of us are communicating, "Don't do what I do; just do as I say." Jesus talked about some people like this. Jesus said, "So you must obey them and do everything they tell you. But do not do what they do, for they do not practice what they preach" (Matt. 23:3). He was referring to the Pharisees. We put ourselves in the same camp as the Pharisees and do not even realize it.

Follow Me As I Follow...

Paul had been a Pharisee before he was saved and had been guilty of telling other people to do what he himself did not do. After his conversion he radically changed his philosophy. Once he had a revelation of the living Christ, he was even bold enough to say, "Follow my example, as I follow the example of Christ" (1 Cor. 11:1).

We, in our desire for humility, say things like, "Don't look at me; follow Christ. I am just a human and can fail too." Of course we do not want to set ourselves up as idols, but I think in reality we do not want to be held accountable for our actions.

By adopting this attitude, we are failing to carry out our God-given responsibility to lead these young ones. If they cannot look to us as role models, to whom will they look?

If they cannot emulate us,
whom will they emulate?
Who will be their heroes?

Many of our young people look up to entertainers

on stage who play loud guitars and have lots of money. Young people think the words of their songs tell them what life is all about. Musicians are today's philosophers.

These Hollywood stars proclaim arrogantly, "Do what I do." Where are the Christians with the backbone to make such a boast? Where are those with such a powerful Christian life that young people who meet them desire to imitate their walk to spiritual maturity? Why do young people have to look to the world to find someone to emulate?

Paul faced many intense situations for the sake of Christ. He was beaten for preaching. He was stoned, whipped and put in jail for his faith. He was hungry, tired, lonely and destitute. He was shipwrecked and bitten by snakes. Then he proclaimed, "Follow me! Just do what I did — imitate me. If you do, you will find your direction in Christ."

Are My Kids More Radical Than I Am?

It is easy to be intimidated by our young people. Though we want them on fire for God, when they get that way we don't know what to do with them. For example, perhaps your teen comes home from school with exciting news about the person he witnessed to that day. "Mom," he says, "I was able to answer all of Tom's questions about God — he really listened to me. We even prayed together, and I was able to help him find Jesus Christ as his personal Savior!"

You know you should be as excited at his news as he is — but you are not. You act as excited as you can and respond, "That is really neat, John," with a big cheesy smile on your face. You try to make it appear that you have that kind of experience every day and end up patronizing him with a "that's-a-good-little-boy" attitude.

In reality you are trying to remember the last time you witnessed to someone. In your heart you are thinking, I wish God would use me like that, or, I wish I was that bold.

Maybe your teen shares how God spoke to her that morning in her quiet time. You knew she was getting up early each morning to seek God, but you didn't realize God was getting up to meet her too. As you listen, you nod your head as if to say, "Isn't that special?" You make it sound as though you have experiences like that every day. In reality you flash back to days of old when you sought God like that and think, Boy, I wish God still spoke to me like that!

Because you do not want your kids to think your spiritual fire has dimmed, you respond condescendingly, "It's great that you are *beginning* to mature in God." Thus you have made their experience seem insignificant.

Many adults lapse into a pattern of imitating a lifestyle on fire for God. They speak the right words and try to express the same zeal as before, but something is missing. Somehow it seems hollow, and none of us wants to admit it. Our passion for God has waned, but we carry the form and do the things we used to do, hoping no one will notice it's gone. We go through the motions trying to get it back.

Our spiritually dynamic kids intimidate us. But instead of getting on our knees and seeking a restoration of intimacy with Christ, we try to make them feel less spiritual than we are. As a result, our kids are not being challenged to continue to grow. It becomes obvious that we are not equipped to challenge them to their next level of growth.

We can observe this phenomenon in some youth groups. Maybe a few teens really get on fire for God. The youth pastor is thrilled but doesn't know what to do to continue challenging them to new spiritual levels. So the well-meaning youth leader concentrates his energies on those who are still not on fire for God. Pretty soon the fired-up ones get bored, thinking they have all there is to get. No one leads them further. Thus many get disillusioned and give up.

How Are You Influencing Them?

As leaders and parents, we are constantly trying to get our kids to do something, to be something, to change something. The essence of leadership is influence, but how do we influence them? What works best?

Many believe concentrated Bible teaching is enough. Others think exciting presentations will do it. But we cannot impact and shape a generation by what we say or preach alone — we influence them with our lives.

Who we are speaks louder than what we say.

It is what we are on the inside that comes screaming through in our relationships with our youth. That is what influences them — good or bad.

The Bible is a sword. As parents we may use that

sword to cut our kids down to size instead of lifting them up with it. As youth leaders we speak the Word, hoping to change them for the better. We come up with teachings we believe are relatable and appropriate, but they lack conviction. "The Word of God will not return void," we say, and justify our lack of preparedness and conviction (Is. 55:11).

This is how our kids hear us sometimes: "Wha-wa? Wha-wa-waa...."

That's right — we sound like Charlie Brown's schoolteacher. We regurgitate some biblical rhetoric and wonder if we really know what we are talking about. Then we ask kids to do things we do not do ourselves. But we don't really expect them to do it either, and the lack of conviction in our voices betrays us.

Our only choice is to ask ourselves some really hard questions: When was the last time I lost all track of time as I prayed? When did I become so engrossed in my Bible that hours passed before I quit? When — if ever — was the last time I fasted?

How are we going to inspire the fire if we do not have the fire?

What happened to those days when we did not care how long a worship service lasted? When did we hunger for righteousness more than anything else? What happened to the radical abandonment that characterized our early days in Christ? When was the last time we read the Bible cover to cover? Have we ever done it? Are we giving from the overflow of the well, or are we scraping the bottom to see if there is anything left to give?

When the fire of the presence of the living God burns in our hearts, our kids will see it. They will be afraid to sin because they know that God will tell us what they did. They will have the confidence that when they discuss a problem with us, we will have an answer from God. Our God-likeness will evoke their immediate respect — not because they are supposed to respect us — but because they see our inner passion for God.

When we know God like this, our influence on our youth is maximized. Our quoted Scriptures are no longer ignored like verbal junk mail. The thunder of our words silences every mocker. When we speak to our kids, they will know that dad or mom just met with God. We no longer try to act spiritual — we are spiritual. *Who we are* backs up *what we say.* We need to make sure we are having our own encounter with God (see chapter 15).

This radical abandonment will free us to communicate more effectively in the pulpit and on the street. If we are radical for Jesus, we will influence others to be radical. But if we are mediocre, we communicate mediocrity. We cannot help it. You can hype it up all you want. You can yell and scream and even act excited. Who you are will still bleed through.

We have a generation to mold — we are here for such a time as this (Esth. 4:14). This generation is waiting for us to *show* them what to do. Let's get on our faces before God and start again where we first began.

INSPIRE THE FIRE!

CHAPTER 5. The Breakdown of Relationships

1. "Teens at high risk for mental illness," *USA Today*, 9 October 1990, p. 1D, quoted in Josh D. McDowell, *Josh McDowell Research Almanac and Statistical Digest* (Julian, Calif.: Julian Press, 1992), p. 309.

2. Marion Winik, "Modern Love," *The American Way*, 1 February 1994, p. 108.

3. "Time: How We Use It, How We Feel About It," *Family Circle*, 27 November 1990, p. 40, quoted in McDowell, *McDowell Research Almanac*, p. 277.

4. Edwin Louis Cole, *Maximized Manhood* (Dallas, Tex.: Whitaker House, 1982), p. 142.

5. "Time: How We Use It," quoted in McDowell, p. 277.

6. Ibid.

7. Anetta Miller, "And What It's Worth," *Newsweek* Special Issue, June 1990, p. 30.

8. David Gelman, "A Much Riskier Passage," *Newsweek* Special Issue, June 1990, p. 16.

9. Ibid, p. 12.

10. Ibid, p. 16.

11. Ibid.

12. Ibid.

13. Eugene C. Roehlkepartain, ed., *Youth Ministry Resource Book* (Loveland, Colo.: Group Publishing, 1988), p. 99, quoted in *High School Evangelism Student Handbook*, Kirk Pankratz, Ray Hollis, Jay Sekulow and Blaine Bartel, eds. (Atlanta: CASE, 1992), p. 32.

14. Marco R. della Cava, "Youths who hit the road often feel unwanted," *USA Today*, 18 October 1989, p. 5D.

15. Robert W. Sweet Jr., *Missing Children: Found Facts*, NIJ Reports, U.S. Department of Justice, report no. 222, November/December 1990, p. 15-18.

16. Bryce Christianson, "Homeless in America," *The Family in America*, a publication of the Rockford Institute Center on the Family in America, June 1990, vol. 4, no. 6, p. 8.

17. Sweet, *Missing Children*, p. 15-18.

18. Daniel Yankelovich, *New Rules* (New York: Bantam Books, 1981/82), pp. 91-94.

19. Patrick Reardon, "Top Threat to Family Is No Time for Kids," *Chicago Tribune*, 10 October 1989, p. 9.

20. *Signs of the Times*, December 1989, p. 6, quoted in McDowell, *McDowell Research Almanac*, p. 250.

21. *Dallas Morning News*, 11 October 1987, p. 34A, quoted in McDowell, *McDowell Research Almanac*, p. 309.

22. "Panel says teens have more health woes today," *San Jose Mercury*, 9 June 1990, p. 1, quoted in McDowell, *McDowell Research Almanac*, p. 311.

23. "New Survey Reveals Shocking Values Among Children," *Educational Newsline*, September/October 1990, p. 1, quoted in McDowell, *McDowell Research Almanac*, p. 310.

24. Marilyn Elias, "Alienation and stress afflict latchkey youth," *USA Today*, 6 September 1990, p. 1D.

25. Nancy Gibb, "How Should We Teach Our Children About SEX?" *Time*, 24 May 1993, p. 61.

26. MTV media kit 1993.

CHAPTER 6. Nothing to Die For

1. David M. Gross & Sophfronia Scott, "Proceeding With Caution," *Time*, 16 July 1990, p. 57.

2. Mary Crystal Cage, "The Post-Baby Boomers Arrive on Campus," *The Chronicle of Higher Education*, 30 June 1993, p. A28.

3. Gross & Scott, "Proceeding With Caution," *Time*, p. 57.

4. John Leland, "Do You Hear What I Hear?" *Newsweek*, 27 January 1992, p. 56.

5. John Leland, "Battle for Your Brain," *Newsweek*, 11 October 1993, p 50.

6. Arthur Levine, "The Making of a Generation," *Change*, September/October 1993, p. 10.

7. Ibid, p. 12.

8. National Center for Health Statistics, 1990 figures.

CHAPTER 7. Competing With the Razzle-Dazzle of the World

1. MTV media kit 1993.

2. McDowell, *Josh McDowell Research Almanac*, p. 229.

CHAPTER 8. How Does God See This Generation?

1. Josh McDowell, *Evidence That Demands a Verdict* (Nashville, Tenn.: Here's Life Publishers, 1979), p. 167.

2. United Nations Demographic Statistics Division, 1993 figures.

3. United Nations Population Trends Division, 1990 figures.

4. Bryant L. Myers, *The Changing Shape of World Missions* (Monrovia, Calif.: MARC [Mission Advanced Research and Communications Center], 1993), p. 40.

CHAPTER 9. Giving Them the Vision

1. John Schwartz, "Stalking the Youth Market," *Newsweek* Special Issue, June 1990, p. 34.

2. Larry Pierce, "Baby Busters: a Lost Generation Finds Its Place in God's Plan," *National and International Religion Report*, (Roanoke, Va.: Media Management, 4 October 1993), p. 1.

3. "What Teens Collect," *Youthviews*, The Newsletter of the Gallup Youth Survey, written by Wendy Plump, based on surveys by Robert Bezilla, January 1994, vol. 1, no. 5, p. 1.

4. Schwartz, "Stalking the Youth Market," *Newsweek*, p. 36.

5. Eugene C. Roehlkepartain, ed., *Youth Ministry Resource Book*, (Loveland, Colo: Group Books, 1988), quoted in *High School Evangelism Student Handbook*, p. 31.

6. Bill Barol, "Anatomy of a Fad," *Newsweek* Special Issue, June 1990, p. 41.

7. Available from Zondervan Publishing House, Grand Rapids, Michigan.

CHAPTER 10. Believing in Their Potential

1. Alexander Star, "The Twentysomething Myth," *The New Republic*, 4 & 11 January 1993, p. 25.

CHAPTER 11. Finding Identity and Belonging in the Call

1. Katrine Ames, "Kids With Causes," *Newsweek* Special Issue, June 1990, p. 64.

2. Gross & Scott, "Proceeding With Caution," *Time*, p. 57.

3. *The 1994 World Book Year Book*, p. 128-137.

CHAPTER 12. The Spiritual Awakening of Teens in the Nineties

1. All Gallup figures from: Robert Bezilla, ed., *America's Youth in the 1990s*, 1st ed. (Princeton, N.J.: The George H. Gallup International Institute, 1993), pp. 153, 155.

2. Figures from the National Center for Educational Statistics, Washington, D.C., March 1994.

3. *Special Report: See You at the Pole 1993*, National Network of Youth Ministries brochure (17150 Via Del Campo, Ste. 102, San Diego, CA 92127, [619] 451-1111), p. 2.

4. Pierce, "Baby Busters," *National and International Religion Report*, p. 3.

5. Ibid, p. 2.

6. *Westside Community Schools v. Mergen*, 495 U.S., 110 L. Ed. 2d (1990).

7. This story is the result of an interview conducted by Fred Carpenter in February 1994.

CHAPTER 14. Preventive Medicine

1. Teen Mania Ministries Acquire the Fire Parents of Teens Questionnaire, 1994.

YOUTH MINISTRY RESOURCES
Printed Materials

1. *Students' Rights and the Public Schools.* 1993. 36 pages. Write: The New American Center for Law & Justice, P.O. Box 64429, Virginia Beach, VA 23467.

2. *The Christian Club Guide.* Randy Brantley & David Hughey. 1991 (2nd edition released, 1994). 120 pages. Write: Christian Club Campaign, c/o Randy Brantley, P.O. Box 552, Little Rock, AR 72203.

3. *A Guide to the Equal Access Act.* Revised edition, 1993. 47 pages. Write: Center for Law and Religious Freedom, 4208 Evergreen Lane, Ste. 222, Annandale, VA 22003.

4. *Take a Stand: Campus Ministry Manual for Students (Condensed Edition).* Compiled by Jeff Swaim. 1993. 32 pages. Write: Youth Alive Campus Ministry, 1445 Boonville Avenue, Springfield, MO 65802.

5. *Youth America Campus Clubs Manual.* Ray Hollis, editor. 1993. 52 pages. Write: Youth America, P.O. Box 20000, Oklahoma City, OK 73156.

6. *The Short Term Mission Handbook.* Berry Publishing Services Inc. 1992. 288 pages. Write: Youth for Christ Project Serve, P.O. Box 228822, Denver, CO 80222, (303) 843-9000.

Other Youth Ministry Organizations

1. Youth With a Mission, North American Office, P.O. Box 55309, Seattle, WA 98155, (206) 363-9844.

2. YUGO Ministries, P.O. Box 25, San Dimas, CA 91773, (714) 592-6621.

3. Calvary Commission, P.O. Box 100, Lindale, TX 75771, (903) 882-5501.

4. DELTA Ministries International, P.O. Box 30029, Portland, OR 97230, (800) 5-DELTA-2.

5. Life Changers, P.O. Box 1103, Decatur, GA 30031, (404) 378-8746.

About the Author

RON LUCE is president and founder of
Teen Mania Ministries, a national youth organization
that takes young people overseas on short-term
missions projects. To date, Teen Mania has taken 5,500
youth to 24 different countries and witnessed over
301,918 people accept Christ. Luce has also developed
the Teen Mania Intern Program, which involves teens in a
full year of discipleship and training.
In addition, Luce hosts Acquire the Fire youth
conventions throughout North America, attracting
thousands of teenagers each weekend.
His ministry has led to guest appearances on
James Dobson's "Focus on the Family" radio broadcast,
"The 700 Club" and Trinity Broadcasting Network.
He is invited to speak at many youth conventions and
Christian colleges across America.
Luce holds a master's degree in counseling
psychology from the University of Tulsa.
He and his wife, Katie, live in Tulsa with their
two daughters, Hannah and Charity.

Teen Mania Ministries conducts conventions across North America called *Acquire the Fire*. If your teen or youth group would like information about how to attend one in your area, please give us a call.

We also take teenagers on summer mission trips for either a four- or eight-week period (we have a two-week trip for groups of fifteen or more to Mexico). We provide all the leadership, meals, travel arrangements, lodging and ministry tools (for example, drama and tracts) so that your teens can be effective in ministry.

Write us today for information on either our summer or Christmas-break trips. We have taken thousands of teens over the years and have documented more than 300,000 people who have given their lives to Jesus through these teens. It is time for your kids to get in on the action!

Contact us at:

Teen Mania Ministries
P.O. Box 700721
Tulsa, OK 74170-0721
(918) 496-1891
(800) 299-TEEN

If you enjoyed *Inspire the Fire*, we would like
to recommend the following books:

Kids Are a Plus
by Ray Mossholder
"Instruct your children in the Lord." Author Ray Mossholder
gives positive instruction on raising your children with a heart
for God. He knows that no parent or child is perfect and that
the Bible must be the road map for life.

Fifty-Six Days Ablaze
by Ron Luce
Fifty-Six Days Ablaze is written especially for teens committed
to learning God's Word and applying it to their lives. This
devotional takes fifteen minutes a day for fifty-six days
(eight weeks) to teach teens what it means to be a
young, excited, committed Christian.

Available at your local Christian bookstore or from:

Creation House
600 Rinehart Road
Lake Mary, FL 32746
1-800-283-7100

Cross Training
by CharismaLife
Ron Luce is a contributing writer to a new life-changing
young teen/youth curriculum called Cross Training. Cross
Training is more than a curriculum; it is a spiritual work-
out that prepares teens to pursue a spiritually aggressive
lifestyle and win the race of life. Available through CharismaLife Publishers. WARNING: This curriculum is radical
and intense. It could cause your youth to focus on Christ
and affect the world for eternity.

For more information call 1-800-451-4598.